Card and po

Theology of
Christian Solidarity

Jon Sobrino, S.J.
Juan Hernández Pico, S.J.

Theology of
Christian Solidarity

Translated from the Spanish
by Phillip Berryman

ORBIS BOOKS
Maryknoll, New York 10545

The Catholic Foreign Mission Society of America (Maryknoll) recruits and trains people for overseas missionary service. Through Orbis Books Maryknoll aims to foster the international dialogue that is essential to mission. The books published, however, reflect the opinions of their authors and are not meant to represent the official position of the society.

Except where otherwise indicated, Bible quotations are from the *New American Bible*. *Bibl. Lat.* = *Biblia Latinoamericana*; NEB = *New English Bible*.

Originally published as, Jon Sobrino, "Conllévaos mutuamente: Análisis teológico de la solidaridad cristiana." *ECA*, San Salvador 401, March 1982, pp. 157–78; and Juan Hernández-Pico, "Conllevar las cargas del reino: Un signo de la unidad eclesial." *Christus*, Mexico City, 554-555, 1982, pp. 59–79. The work was subsequently published as *Teología de la solidaridad cristiana*, copyright © 1983, by the Instituto Histórico Centroamericano, Apdo. A-194, Managua, Nicaragua, and the Centro Ecuménico Antonio Valdivieso, Apdo. 3205, Managua, Nicaragua.

English translation copyright © 1985 by Orbis Books, Maryknoll, NY 10545

Manuscript Editor: William E. Jerman

Library of Congress Cataloging in Publication Data

Sobrino, Jon.
  Theology of Christian solidarity.

  Translation of: Teologia de la solidaridad cristiana.
  Bibliography: p.
  1. Solidarity—Resigious aspects—Christianity—
Addresses, essays, lectures.   I. Hernández Pico, Juan.
II. Title.
BT738.45.S6313   1985   261.8'097284   84-16533
ISBN 0-88344-452-6 (pbk.)

CONTENTS

PROEM

For the past few years
one of the words heard most often
in Central America,
and throughout the world, regarding Central America,
has been "solidarity":
solidarity with El Salvador,
solidarity with Nicaragua,
solidarity with Guatemala,
solidarity with Central America.

Solidarity is another name for the kind of love
that moves feet, hands, hearts,
material goods, assistance, and sacrifice
toward the pain, danger, misfortune, disaster, repression,
or death
of other persons
or a whole people.
The aim is to share with them
and help them rise up, become free,
claim justice, rebuild.

In the pain, misfortune, oppression,
and death
of the people,
God is silent.
God is silent on the cross,
in the crucified.
And this silence is God's word,
God's cry.

In solidarity God speaks the language of love.
God makes a statement,
utters a self-revelation,
and takes up a presence
in solidarity.

God is love,
God stands in solidarity,
God is solidarity.
Where there is solidarity,
there is God,
making an efficacious statement.

And everything God says
—in speech, in silence, in stridency—
is to seek solidarity,
greater solidarity.

In Central America God is speaking through solidarity.
God speaks where there is solidarity with Central America.
And God calls for solidarity with Central America,
with its peoples,
with the suffering poor.

Jon Sobrino, S.J.

BEARING WITH ONE
ANOTHER IN FAITH

The New Phenomenon of Christian Solidarity

The early 1980s witnessed a growing movement of solidarity toward Christians and churches in Latin America. Because it is something new and yet quite sizeable, this solidarity deserves study. Such a study ought to involve an analysis of what has actually happened so as to be able to define in Christian terms what solidarity means; it also ought to uncover the deepest roots of solidarity; and it ought to clarify what the rediscovery of solidarity means for the church and for faith.

The reflections I offer here are based on the solidarity shown toward the people and the church of El Salvador, and so they bear the limitations inherent in any particular case study. On the other hand, I believe the solidarity shown toward El Salvador is an eloquent case history in the contemporary life of the church and quite sufficient for working out some theoretical guidelines for what might be called a "theology of solidarity." In any case, these reflections are based on solidarity as it has actually appeared and not on an a priori and merely conceptual formulation.

On a descriptive level what I wish to stress is first the immense movement of solidarity toward the people and the

1

church of El Salvador. Many individuals and institutions have made the church of El Salvador their "neighbor" in the gospel meaning of the term: they have not taken a detour in order to avoid seeing the wounded victim on the road, but instead have come closer to examine the situation and to help. Cardinals, archbishops, bishops, priests, and religious men and women of the Catholic Church, delegations from Protestant churches, and theologians both Catholic and Protestant have come to this country. Many professional politicians, journalists, jurists, members of human rights organizations and aid agencies have also come and many of them in addition to their professional capacity have shown their specific concern as Christians. They have carried out their visit in a Christian way, engaging in dialogue with church personnel, taking part in meetings and liturgical celebrations with other Christians, and, most of all, coming close to suffering Salvadorans in the countryside, in jails, and in refugee camps.

Many others who could not come here have nevertheless from afar made the Salvadoran church really their "neighbor." There have been countless letters from grassroots Christian communities from all over the world, especially from Latin American rural and urban workers and Amerindians belonging to such communities, as well as from priests, religious, academics, and professional persons. Bishops from various countries and sometimes whole episcopal conferences have made official statements denouncing the repression, the violation of human rights, and the persecution of the church, and they have supported the guidelines given by Archbishops Romero and Rivera, encouraging the poor to keep up their hope and to remain steadfast in their just struggles. Groups of theologians have signed and sent letters of solidarity, circulated theological and pastoral writings emerging from Central America, and offered their own thinking to shed light on Central American problems. Many institutions have sent material aid for the poor and persecuted, for refugees and exiles, and also for social and humanitarian works of the church, and for its communications media. Persons in many countries of Europe and the Americas have organized solidarity committees in order to receive and share reliable information, raise funds, pressure their governments, and organize liturgies and solidarity demonstrations.

Finally there are those who have come from outside and have stayed close to their "neighbor," working in isolated parishes and aiding the suffering population in pastoral, humanitarian, and theological ways. As a symbol of this kind of solidarity we may recall those who have remained forever at the side of the people as martyrs. The martyrdom of the four women missionaries from the United States and of priests who have come from other countries is the supreme expression of their really coming close and giving all.

What first strikes the eye in this vast movement of solidarity is the aid that other Christians and other churches have offered the Salvadoran church. Nevertheless, in order to describe correctly what has happened and to adequately work out a theological concept of solidarity we must analyze more deeply what is behind this phenomenon and delineate how it differs from other phenomena that seem to be similar to solidarity but, strictly speaking, are not expressions of solidarity.

Solidarity of this sort is not mere humanitarian "aid," of the kind that often is prompted by natural disasters, for example. That kind of aid is obviously good and necessary and is a correct response to an ethical imperative. But if solidarity were no more than material aid, it would not be anything more than a magnified kind of almsgiving where givers offer something they own without thereby feeling a deep-down personal commitment or without feeling any need to continue this aid. In authentic solidarity the first effort to give aid commits a person at a deeper level than that of mere giving and becomes an ongoing process, not a contribution.

Moreover, when the initial aid is given, the giving and receiving churches set up relationships. It is not a matter of a one-way flow of aid but of mutual giving and receiving. This point enables us to get closer to what solidarity actually means, but again we must clarify what is specific to the kinds of relationships that solidarity creates between churches.

One could think of solidarity along the lines of an "alliance" between different churches to better defend their own interests, along the lines of solidarity as conceived in politics.

But this idea would not explain the true origin of ecclesial solidarity; it has not been generated by the self-interest of a particular church but rather in order to help the "other" church, which itself has turned to the "others," the poor, the oppressed, the suffering. Hence solidarity is not an alliance formed to defend one's own interests, even though through solidarity many churches are discovering what their true interests ought to be. If the alliance model were the real basis for understanding solidarity, the ultimate judgment on it would have to be that it was simply a matter of ecclesiastical self-centeredness, whether because the interests of the churches as a whole were given priority over the interests of the poor, or because one church sought its own advantage in helping another church. But neither of these approaches is what has actually given rise to solidarity.

If it is not simply aid from one church to another nor an alliance between different churches in order to promote their interests, what is the specific element in solidarity? Further on we shall analyze this point in a more detailed way. At this stage it would be well for us to single out the elements that have set solidarity in motion in recent history so as to bring out what is specific in solidarity when seen from a Christian viewpoint: (1) Solidarity has been set in motion when some churches help another church that is in need because it has taken on solidarity with the poor and oppressed among its own people. (2) These helping churches find out that they not only give but also receive from the church they aid. What they receive is of a different and higher order; they usually describe it as new inspiration in faith and help in discovering their identities in human, ecclesial, and Christian terms and in relationship to God. (3) Through mutual giving and receiving the churches establish relationships and make the discovery that in principle it is essential that a local church be united to another church and that in principle this mutual relationship embraces all levels of life, from material aid to faith in God.

This new way for Christians and the churches to be related (a matter of both fact and principle), which starts with the basic solidarity of the church with its poor and oppressed, is maintained as a process of mutual giving and receiving and is raised to the level of faith (although it takes its origins from ethical practices carried out in ongoing history)—this is what is meant by solidarity. This is the way for Christians and churches to relate to one another in accordance with the well-known Pauline admonition, "Bear with one another." This is a conception of Christian life and a way of practicing it in which reference to "the other" is essential, both in giving and in receiving, both on the human level and on ecclesial and Christian levels, and the level of relationship with God, both in seeing in the other the ethical demand of responsibility and in finding graciousness in that other. Solidarity is therefore the Christian way to overcome, in principle, individualism, whether personal or collective, both at the level of our involvement in history and on the level of faith.

The Origin of Solidarity: The Fact of the Poor

The root of solidarity as I have thus far described it is something both real in history and effective. By "real in history" I mean that the present form of solidarity has not been set in motion by an effort of the will or by imposition from above, as if solidarity were something good "in itself" and therefore to be practiced. By "effective" I mean that what has happened in El Salvador and elsewhere is of such a magnitude that it has been able to emancipate many churches from their centuries-old isolation.

The objective fact we are speaking of, which is both real in history and effective, is the fact of misery, oppression, and injustice in which millions of human beings live. The unveiling of this truth has amounted to a revelation for many persons elsewhere, including Christians, and they have felt questioned and challenged by this objective reality. The truth of the poor has therefore made its appearance and many have grasped this truth and reacted appropriately.

There are two aspects to this discovery that, although they are related, should be distinguished if we are to understand solidarity: (1) what has occasioned the discovery of the truth of the poor (the genetic focus, a question of fact); (2) what has actually been uncovered (the systematic focus, a question of principle).

The Disclosure

From a purely genetic viewpoint what began to attract worldwide attention and set in motion initial solidarity was the fact that some churches took up a stance vis-à-vis the world of the poor and accepted the consequences of that stance. What is involved is the kind of solidarity that is constitutive of a church and is prior to solidarity between churches, although it is basic to it: service in solidarity offered to the world of the poor. What has happened is that the desire of Medellín that "the church in Latin America be one that evangelizes the poor and stands in solidarity with them" (Poverty of the Church) has become a reality.

The Disclosed

It is clear that it was the murder of priests in 1977 that first drew attention to what was going on in El Salvador, because it provided the news media with something different. This spectacular fact served to uncover the persecution (unfortunately less spectacular and newsworthy) of the rural and urban poor, pastoral ministers, grass-roots Christian communities, and church institutions. In a word, the persecution of the church became known. (See e.g., Martin Lange and Reinhold Iblacker, eds., *Witnesses of Hope: The Persecution of Christians in Latin America,* Maryknoll, N.Y., Orbis, 1981.)

This cruel and public persecution led to questions about the causes behind it or, in other words, to the mission of the church that brought persecution to it. Even though the answer had been known on a theoretical level, the reality of this mission finally broke through to many thoughtful observers: it was the overall liberation of human beings who live in inhuman conditions, whose most elemental human rights are utterly violated, and who are repressed in all their just strivings for liberation.

Persecution of the church therefore had two important effects. The first, which was more immediate and evident, was incipient solidarity with a persecuted church; the second, less apparent at first but deeper and more important in the long run, was the unveiling of the fact of the poor, of their situation and their future.

In the order of logic, coming to know the truth of the poor is independent of knowing what happens to the church. But for many Christians (and in general for persons of good will everywhere) the persecution of the church has been decisive in their discovery of the truth of the poor. If even the church is repressed and its priests are murdered, then it becomes quite credible that such is also the lot of the poor. What is worse and more tragic, the anonymous poor will be repressed with even fewer scruples and misgivings than those shown toward the church as a public institution. Moreover, because it was newsworthy the persecution of the church brought to the attention of the world images, testimonies, and commentaries on the horror of repression. In this way the truth of the poor was communicated in a way that went beyond dispassionate narration; it managed to reach levels of feeling. The truth of the poor was not only made known; it unleashed indignation and protest. Finally, because it is the church that is persecuted and communicates the oppression and repression of the people through its own persecution, this truth is automatically presented as an ethical demand on others. The truth of the poor thus unveiled requires a response not only with a theoretical judgment but with a practical judgment that sets in motion some form of concrete action.

In sum, the truth of the poor, already known theoretically and often affirmed by the church, became a truth that was "more real," "more the truth," when it was proclaimed credibly by a persecuted church. Furthermore, it was proclaimed as a truth that must not only be registered in conscience but as a truth demanding a reaction.

This genesis of solidarity in ongoing history is thus an example of a common phenomenon: what comes first on the level of reality comes last on the level of knowledge, and vice versa. The levels of knowledge and reality as regards the situation in Central America are diagrammed in Figure 1, page 8.

level of knowledge	FIGURE 1	
	socio-political fact	level of reality
level of knowledge		**level of reality**
1	murder of priests	5
↓		↑
2	persecution of the church	4
↓		↑
3	repression of the people	3
↓		↑
4	overall wretchedness	2
↓		↑
5	structural oppression	1

On the level of knowledge what has set solidarity in motion has been the harassment and even murder of priests and of at least one bishop, Archbishop Romero of San Salvador. Nevertheless, on the level of (antecedent) reality, the sequence is the reverse. Awareness of these two levels or sequences is instructive both for individuals and for churches seeking to follow out the dictates of their faith.

When persons have correctly grasped the two sequences for what they are in reality, then they are ready to sink deep roots in the movement of solidarity, including the dimensions of that movement relating to the church and to God.

In principle, the discovery of the reality of the poor is the origin of solidarity because this truth is a primal call to the human dimension within any person and a challenge based on the fact that each of us is socially a part of all humankind. It brings with it a demand for change and conversion, for persons to recover their true identity underlying a falsified identity. And it provides the opportunity to recover this identity through co-responsibility for the poor.

In theological terms, the basic issue is ultimately that in many places it has become clear that God's order of creation is threatened, debased, and repudiated. This elemental truth is often soft-pedaled or passed over in silence or, in any case, presented in such an undynamic way that it does not really register in personal or collective awareness. But concerned individuals and groups made it their business to dissipate deceptive smoke screens and "call a spade a spade."

The true condition of the poor has been discovered, documented, and disseminated. Their cry has not only gone up to heaven, but has made itself heard around the earth. Many men and women in Central America and elsewhere in the world are dying the slow death of oppression or the quick death of repression. This is the most basic fact in the world today—and it is a fact utterly in defiance of God's will.

This basic fact is a challenge to the very idea of humankind and its intrinsic unity. This fact unmasks the understanding of humanness imposed on others by analogy to its assumed "superior" Western prime analogue—the modern human being living in an affluent society, *the* human being.

The facts belie this facile assumption. The bulk of humankind is made up of poor persons whose lives are seriously threatened at basic levels. In comparison to them, the so-called modern human being of affluent societies is an exception. Taking the exception as the *analogatum princeps* of the human being is at least questionable. Those who want to maintain this position ought to recognize that Western humanity is the exception in the order of logic—and ask themselves whether it is not also the exception in the order of causality: Is the exceptional life of some perhaps due to the large-scale exploitation or death of others?

Seen in this light, the unity of humankind cannot be conceived in an idealist fashion as participation in the monolithic essence of what it means to be human, nor can the differences among human beings be explained simply in terms of different degrees of participation in the being of Western humanness. Much less may the differences be put forward (at least initially) as differences that are enriching and hence to be taken into account for planning a unified humankind. At present humankind is not simply differentiated but deeply divided. The basic difference is between being close to life or close to death, between affluent societies where life and the most basic rights of the human person are safeguarded, and societies where misery, blatant violation of human rights, and death prevail. What makes this division especially critical is that these differences do not simply coexist; they stand in a mutual cause-and-effect relationship.

Co-responsibility

Our reflection up to this point unavoidably simplifies matters, but it was important in order to understand the roots of solidarity. The unveiling of the de facto condition of the poor has served to force individuals and groups to reformulate the question of what constitutes the most basic problem in human history and the most basic division between human beings. It has served to relativize and unmask the Western world, which with its penchant for autonomy, development, and abundance, has been taken to be the model of what is human and civilized.

Most of all, this unveiling has served to lead many to feel questioned and challenged in the social dimension of their personality, beyond the social aspect touching on family, civic, church, and national groupings. To put it most concisely, they have come to seriously question what it means to be a human being in this divided humankind where some live and others die, where the life of some partly depends on the death of others, and vice versa. The co-responsibility that must be shouldered if human beings are to be fully human has thereby been accentuated. The unveiling of the situation of the poor has prompted believers to reformulate and rethink the question of their faith in God, again at the most basic levels of life, beyond a faith simply imbibed from their ambient culture or one that merely tries to survive the threat posed by unbelief. It has served to make these basic realities a mediation of the question of God and the response to the mystery of God. Put simply, it has served to integrate into the nucleus of faith God's question to Cain, "What has become of your brother?" And it makes a positive answer to this question a fundamental mediation of the practice of faith.

This response to the suffering of the poor is an ethical demand, but it is also a practice that is salvific for those who enter into solidarity with the poor. Those who do so often recover in their own life the deep meaning they thought they had lost; they recover their human dignity by becoming integrated into the pain and suffering of the poor. From the poor they receive, in a way they hardly expected, new eyes for seeing the ultimate truth of things and new energies for exploring unknown and dangerous paths. For them the poor are "others," and when they take on solidarity with them they undergo the experience of being sent to others only to find their own truth. At the very moment of giving they find themselves expressing gratitude for something new and better that they have been given. It is not difficult to recognize that what the poor provide insofar as they are "others" is a mediation of God's gratuitousness. But whether this gratuitousness is explicitly referred back to God or remains unidentified, it is clear that in aiding the poor one receives from them meaning for one's own life. In this manner the initial aid becomes solidarity—giving and receiving, bearing with one another.

The root of solidarity is accordingly to be found in what generates human co-responsibility, makes co-responsibility an imperious ethical demand, and makes the exercises of co-responsibility something good, fulfilling, and salvific.

The role of the church in setting this solidarity in motion has been twofold. First, in a more instrumental way, the church has played a positive role in helping others come to know the truth of the poor majority, so that those who are not poor will not, in Paul's phrase, "imprison the truth with injustice," but rather come to recognize the tragic situation of the majority of humankind as the bottommost fact of our present history. The church has been an instrument for giving voice to the cry of the poor majority, who by their very existence are trumpeting the proclamation that today one cannot be a human being *and* disregard the sufferings of millions of other human beings.

Secondly, to the extent that the church has itself become a church of the poor, it has become a real symbol of the poor, not only pointing to their truth from outside, but expressing that truth within itself. A church incarnate in the world of the poor, that defends their destiny and shares in their lot of persecution and death, visibly manifests the reality of the poor of the world.

In this way the church shows how it can and must be church today and what its identity is. But it also shows how one can and must be human today and which road leads toward the utopia of a united humankind: it begins by turning to the poor and bearing their poverty. Such a church is one that dissolves isolation between churches and helps to dissolve isolation between the world of the poor and the world of those who live in affluence. But the root of this desegregation and positive solidarity is to be found in the first and basic solidarity, solidarity with the poor of this world.

Solidarity as the Basic Way for Churches to Relate to One Another

The church's turn toward the world of the poor, whether in the universal church or in a particular local church, is the basic solidarity of the church, that with which it carries out its mission and maintains its identity. Moreover, it is this basic solidarity that begins to dissolve the isolation of local churches and establish new, positive relationships between local churches. On the basis of this fact—and always keeping in mind its roots in de facto history—it is possible to reformulate and better solve a series of theoretical problems regarding the essence and history of the church—problems with important practical consequences. These problems touch on the relationship of the churches with one another and the relationship between the different confessions. I am going to focus here concretely on the catholicity of the church, missionary aid from one church to another, and the ecumenical movement. I believe these three issues can be formulated better from the angle of solidarity.

The catholicity of the church, which has always been held to be one of the essential notes of the true church, means that there is one universal church realized in the multiplicity of local churches. There is only one church because there is only one God, only one Christ, and only one Spirit. This is what demands and guarantees the unity of the church. Inasmuch as this, rather than something created, is the ultimate root of unity, the church should in principle have the capacity to extend to different places and take on the peculiar features of those places. If such were not the case—if only certain places, certain situations, or certain cultures were suitable for the embodiment of the church—it would amount to a forceful denial of the transcendent origin of the church and would set quantitative and qualitative limits to what God can do. The true church is inherently both universal and local.

We have here in this theoretical formulation the problem of the one and the many, and how to combine them. It is very important to know which theoretical model is used to resolve the problem. Very serious practical consequences are at stake. Three theoretical models—none of which may be perfectly verified in the concrete—have been used to explain the nature and functioning of the church: (1) uniformity, (2) pluralism, and (3) solidarity.

The Uniformity Model

The theoretical model of uniformity presupposes that the essence of the church exists prior to its concrete embodiments. Catholicity means that different local churches share in this essence. The model recognizes a minimum of diversity in this participation—diversity resulting from historical and cultural differences in local churches. In the best interpretation of this model such differences are regarded as possible enrichments of the overall composition of the universal church. But in practice the tendency was always to minimize differences, and the ideal proposed was that of the greatest possible similarity between local churches.

This model was the one in effect in the Catholic Church in the years prior to Vatican II. In the name of the universality of the church the tendency was to encourage (sometimes through imposition by administrative means) not only the same doctrine and the same morality, but also the same liturgy, the same administrative policies, the same theology, and even the same philosophy. The tension inherent in catholicity was broken in favor of universality and of the greatest possible resemblance between churches. This of course led to absurdities. To give just one example, seminarians all over the world studied philosophy from manuals written with a nineteenth-century mentality and published in Spain. The element of ecclesial localness disappeared. In this model there was no allowance for positive and mutually enriching relationships between local churches. They were merely set alongside one another and there was little to differentiate one from another as churches. This was seen as the ideal to be pursued for the sake of church unity.

The Pluriformity Model

The uniformity model fell apart in both theory and practice at the time of Vatican II. It ceded place to pluralism. The emphasis was now, in principle, on the necessity and importance of the local element in the church, diversity in liturgical, pastoral, and theological expressions was encouraged. This diversity was understood as being an enrichment for the universal church. There was no reason why diversity should threaten church unity; in fact it could only enhance that unity.

Nevertheless, two important factors are missing from the pluralist model—and even more to say from the uniformity model.

The first is that the localness of a church—that is, its character as formed by historical, economic, social, and political factors—is given virtually no ecclesial importance. In other words, no importance is given to the concrete world in which the church is incarnate. Nor is adequate consideration given to the need for a church to be incarnate in misery and poverty as basic elements of its localness, or for the need of a church to specify and concretize its mission in accordance with these down-to-earth realities. These realities do not figure in either the uniformity or pluriformity models as mediations for faith, for the following of Jesus, for building the church. It is not clear in them how the fundamental differences resulting from milieus of misery and of affluence, and the new responses of churches to these situations, can be seen as enriching the new liturgy, new pastoral practices, and the theology flowing from them.

The second thing missing is that, although pluralism is legitimized in order to do justice to the local church and to enrich the universal church, there is no provision for relating local churches directly—and urgently—to one another. In other words, in this model there is no way for decisively introducing co-responsibility between churches, mutual giving and receiving, bearing with one another, as a form of catholicity. Therefore, the pluralist model, although legitimate and necessary in itself, and although it marks an advance over the uniformity model, does not get much beyond being a legitimate demand (in the liberal mold) that the right of local churches to autonomy be recognized.

The Solidarity Model

The third possibility is to understand catholicity in terms of solidarity between different local churches. In the tension between universality and localness, the latter is given preference for the sake of authentic Christian universality.

To begin with, catholicity means co-responsibility between local churches. Mutual love is seen as the essential and primary element for relating local churches with one another and unifying them. This loving co-responsibility is achieved through the mutual giving and receiving of churches to and from one another. This giving and receiving should be extended to diverse areas of the life of the church: liturgical, pastoral, and theological, but based on something yet more fundamental: giving and receiving in the practice of faith. Catholicity thus means bearing with one another in faith.

This bearing with one another in faith should not be understood in a formal and abstract sense but as practiced in the concrete. That is why it is all-important to determine what practice of faith it is that actually sets in motion this bearing with one another in faith. Such practice should include responding to God's will regarding the life and death of human beings. Solidarity between churches therefore presupposes that somewhere in the universal church there is ecclesial solidarity with the poor. That is how bearing with one another is practiced today.

Catholicity understood as co-responsibility is not an obstacle to the universality of the church, but rather helps to build it up. If this co-responsibility penetrates to the level of faith, the catholicity of the church is simply the building up of the faith of the universal church in history, a faith made up of pluriform and different faiths. Bearing with one another in faith is how the faith of the one church is embodied in ways that are related to ongoing history, differentiated and complementary. In no way does this deny that in the church there are universal levels and procedures for judging different expressions of faith. But these levels and procedures do not create the reality of the universal faith, which is built up when there is a genuine readiness for giving and receiving the faith to and from one another. Unity in the content of the faith is guaranteed by the magisterium of the church; but unity in embodying faith in that content is made effective when faith interacts with faith.

Within the universal church at particular moments there are some local churches that are privileged. It would be a mistake to think of the universal church simply as an agglomeration of all the local churches, with no one of them more important for the universal church at a particular moment. However it is to be explained, at certain periods one local church better incarnates the suffering of humankind, better announces the good news to the poor, denounces sin more clearly, suffers persecution more than other churches do, and gives the witness of supreme love in martyrdom; in a word, it better carries out the mission and embodies the essence of the church, is more clearly seen to be the sacrament of salvation, and gives greater witness of faith in God, in Christ, and in the Spirit.

As a result, some local churches are a leaven for the whole church—as the church should be leaven for the world—and these local churches should be seen as occasions of grace for the universal church. Naturally, this in no way gives such churches any reason to be arrogant, but it does demand that the universal church not overlook these occasions of grace and certainly that it should not reject them, but rather that it should turn its eyes to these churches. That is where it will more easily find God's will through the signs of the times, and also learn how to respond to them.

I hope that these reflections will aid in understanding a little better what the catholicity of the church is, and how important it is. Catholicity means direct co-responsibility between local churches, giving and receiving the best they have, teaching and learning their most valid insights, bearing with one another. At particular moments there emerge privileged churches that set this process in motion. It is their right to do so because they embody better the essence and mission of the church. It is when this process takes place that the universal church is built up and the unity of the church is made real in history. The foundation and ultimate guarantee of this unity is transcendent: God, Christ, and the Spirit. But unity in history is based on incarnating this faith—that is why it is all-important to examine where this faith is best being incarnated—and on doing so together, "bearing with one another in faith."

Mission

A concrete and important form of catholicity is missionary activity. Traditionally, "to engage in mission" means going to other places to announce the faith to non-Christians and founding local churches. Here, however, I understand by missionary activity the sending of "missionaries" (even if they do not refer to themselves that way) from local churches in the First World to local churches in Latin America in order to help extend and strengthen the faith in our churches, which suffer from a shortage of priests, sisters, and lay pastoral ministers. And I understand this activity as solidarity—that is, as the way that local churches of the First World and those of Latin America bear with one another on the basic level of faith.

In a number of First World churches, and certainly in the most perceptive, the meaning and purpose of sending "missionaries" to Latin America has become a problem. One indication of it is that different orders and congregations in the United States that send religious to the Third World have had to hold conferences on the issue.

Part of the problem comes from the danger (and often the fact) of neocolonialism and domination. Although this prob-

lem is serious, there is in theory an answer for how to overcome it: acculturation and an attitude of service. Nevertheless, I believe that at a deeper level the difficulty demands
answers to two questions arising out of missionary activity
itself and not simply *how* it is carried out: (1) What does it
mean to engage in mission in Latin America today?
(2) What does it mean to be sent unilaterally to provide a service? Although they are expressed here in an abstract manner,
these questions arise out of the experience of missionaries
and the churches that have sent them. Let us examine them in
some detail so as to see how the solidarity model may aid in
answering them.

The problem involved in the first question may be expressed as follows. Missionaries come in order to communicate the faith they already have, the faith already embodied in
their local church, and indeed it could not be otherwise. They
come in order to communicate generously what they have—
their faith. The question that arises is whether this faith—
inevitably in the concrete form of the faith of a local
church—is adequate for doing missionary work in Latin
America. Furthermore, the aim one has in announcing the
faith to others depends on how one understands the faith. To
put it very simply, the missionary—or any Christian—faces
this question: Does the faith that I possess at this point give
me any reason to communicate it to others?

Two basic answers, different but complementary, can be
given to this question. The first, more traditional, reply is that
faith is communicated so that others, as individuals, may
come to possess faith or have it strengthened. This is the understanding of mission as the gaining of converts, in a positive, not pejorative, meaning of the term. The second answer
is that faith is communicated so that the kingdom of God may
become a reality. In this view mission is understood as
evangelization, in the sense the term has for Isaiah and
Jesus—that is, liberation. Logically, the first line of missionary activity would emphasize the truth of what is an-
nounced; the second would rather emphasize putting love
into practice. The question then put to the missionary, and
particularly to one coming from a distant environment, is

how to fit together these two notions of "doing mission."

We now turn to the problem involved in the second question. When First World churches send missionaries, they are providing a service, they are "giving" of what they have, sometimes the best they have, and along with missionaries they provide other resources of all kinds. Missionary activity thus formally consists in "giving." But by their own experience they know that besides giving they also receive from the churches that are the object of mission; they know that they, as First World churches, give out of their manifold abundance, but that they also receive from the poverty of the churches to which they are sent in mission.

Hence the question: Is it correct to see mission as a one-way service of one church to another? Is it enough to understand missionary activity as the unidirectional sending of missionaries? Putting it more sharply, can we correctly understand missionary activity today without a prior willingness to be the object of mission from those to whom mission is directed? It is a Christian truth that one who gives receives, and throughout history many missionaries have expressed their gratitude for how much they received when they engaged in mission. The question here, however, is structural rather than personal: Are local sending churches willing to receive from mission-receiving churches?

These questions are not abstract but concrete. They are questions posed by mission-sending churches of the First World, which are in fact member churches of the same universal church that subsists in Latin American churches—churches in the world of the poor. In this concrete situation, answers to the questions posed above can be framed in terms of missionary activity conceived as solidarity, as mission-sending and mission-receiving churches bearing with one another.

The framework of solidarity broadens the focus on missionary activity as moving only in one direction. In the concrete, sending missionaries means the service of one local church to another, but also the possibility that the mission-sending church may be evangelized by the mission-receiving church. In this formulation mission is a positive concept for both mission-receiving churches of the Third World and mission-sending churches of the First World.

When missionaries are sent not only to respond formally to the mandate that there be missionary activity and not only as an expresssion of the generosity of a local church (although this is very important), but also with the awareness of their own need to be evangelized, "overseas" missions become very important for the local sending church. When persons go to an "overseas" mission and bring its reality back to the First World—in their writings or other forms of communication—or when they return temporarily or permanently, then their First World church acquires a new principle for its own growth. This principle is simply the admission of the presence of the poor into the First World church so that it may find a broadened Christian way to its own conversion, its own faith, its own ecclesial mission. To set out to engage in missionary activity "with all the consequences" will shatter the one-way image of mission and view it instead as solidarity.

This conception of mission modifies and completes the theological notion of sending. Missionaries are sent by their own church to other churches, and this sending ultimately derives from God. It is God who sends, and hence all missionary activity has an essential component "from above." However, if mission is conceived as solidarity, then missionaries are re-sent to their original local churches by the poor of Latin America. This sending has no canonical status but it is no less real on that account. It is a sending from the poor, "from below."

Solidarity thus introduces a circularity into the theological category of sending. In de facto experience that is the way it has often happened; many missionaries who come to preach the faith of their sending churches later return to them with the faith of the poor with whom they have worked in mission. But the circularity is also theological, given the twofold presence of God, both in the institutional aspects of the church and in the poor. In the former, God is present with the mandate to "go to all nations"; in the latter, God is present evangelizing from the side of the poor. Therefore sending cannot be adequately understood in a one-way sense. Christian will-ingness of local churches to send missionaries entails an openness to having them sent back by the poor churches of Latin America.

A circular understanding of sending is an aid in carrying out missionary activity as solidarity—that is, as not only giv-ing but also receiving. With this point we have clarified the second question posed above. We now have to answer the first: What does it mean to engage in mission in Latin America? In my view, answering this question means taking seriously the one who is to be evangelized. The one at whom evangelization is aimed is not simply the "person" nor is it the "pagan"—it is ultimately the "poor person." According to Christian faith, the poor are the privileged object of God's love and Jesus' ministry. If we take this correlation with utter seriousness, if we accept with utter seriousness that God loves the poor just because they are poor, and that Jesus an-nounced the good news directly to the poor, then it is from the vantage point of the poor that the missionary will best understand the content of evangelization and the best way to evangelize. This is valid for the missionary's own faith as well as for his or her missionary activity.

Simply by being poor and having the theological signifi-cance we have noted, the poor person is, for the missionary, first of all a question and a challenge. That person is not just someone ignorant who must be taught, but someone from whom (or at least through whom) the missionary must learn what is most basic in the Christian faith. The poor person re-lativizes the missionary's knowledge, despite whatever prior knowledge he or she may have possessed. The poor person's abundance of not-knowing, which may make the missionary uncomfortable, is nevertheless the precondition for con-cretely putting into practice what the missionary knows. In a word, and stating it in a radical form, the otherness of the poor person provides the not-knowing that is essential for knowing God. This otherness, however, because it is the otherness of the poor person and not simply of someone else like the missionary, drives one back to God's otherness in a manner that is specifically Christian. We shall not arrive at

God's otherness simply by extrapolating what we already know of God, but rather in discontinuity from what we already know of God. The poor person is the one who in de facto history relativizes and even contradicts what missionaries coming from affluent countries believe they already know of God. Accepting this relativization and contradiction brings missionaries to a better knowledge of God. The same could be said of other basic contents of the Christian faith such as Christ, the church, love, truth, and so forth.

When missionaries have been taught the faith, they then understand what it means to communicate it to the poor and how to maintain the tension between announcing the faith so it may be believed (making converts) and practicing the faith (building up the kingdom of God). To be a missionary to the Latin American poor means proclaiming to them the truth of God and Christ and making real what they want in a manner that is both dialectical and unified, in such a way that announcing the faith moves toward the practice of the kingdom and that the practice from within itself clarifies the content of the proclamation.

This complementarity could conceivably be discovered in an unhistorical manner by analyzing the texts of revelation, but it is in fact discovered when persons go to engage in mission with the poor. The discovery in ongoing history is what has made it possible to discover such complementarity in revelation. The proclamation of God's truth so that it may be believed is important because it is the truth, but also because this truth not only speaks of salvation but, once it is pronounced, it also becomes an integral, salvific element in history. The practice of the kingdom of God is important because it is a Christian exigency—and in Latin America an exigency that is urgent and indispensable; but that practice is also important because it sheds light on God's truth as believed.

It is the poor who make possible in history the synthesis between announcing God's truth and incarnating God's kingdom, between announcing Christ and following Jesus, between truth and charity, between proselytism to increase the number of believers and deepen their faith, and work for liberation. When missionaries from abroad take with utter seriousness the fact that the object of their mission is the poor person, then they begin to understand the reason for coming to Latin America and what it means to engage in mission.

Missionary activity is therefore solidarity between local churches. We have already hinted at what the poor give to mission-sending churches. Obviously they have "neither gold nor silver" to offer. But when they send missionaries back to their local churches, the poor offer their own poverty as a questioning of the way that being human is understood and as another possible way to be human. When the poor live their poverty with spirit, with gospel values, with courage in persecution, with hope in their struggles, with the kind of love that can sustain martyrdom, what they are offering is simply their faith.

They also offer, not for rote imitation but to serve as inspiration, the Christian creativity that poverty with spirit generates: new pastoral and liturgical experimentation, grassroots community enterprises, new forms of lay ministry, new modes of theological reflection. All this they offer gratefully to those who help them from outside.

What mission-sending churches offer has also been suggested. They provide all kinds of necessary resources. They send missionaries, many of whom work resolutely, some to the point of offering their life in martyrdom. They offer the humility of respecting the values of others and learning from the faith of others. When they do all this, what they are offering is simply their faith.

Moreover, under present circumstances, solidarity with Latin America and the sending of missionaries constitute a kind of reparation by First World countries for what was done in the past. Mission as here portrayed is not only a Christian obligation, it is also an obligation derived from history: reparation for other kinds of church involvement and political intervention of an enslaving nature. Solidarity cemented by mission becomes a small and indeed utopian sign of how relationships between the First World and Latin America should be. For the "vital interests of an empire" they substitute the interests inherent in the life of the poor. The service that missionary solidarity renders here is not slight— although, admittedly, it is utopian—when it shows how international relationships can be mutually beneficial and when it denounces types of "aid" that are nothing but intervention. At least some churches will stand out as a sign of true international solidarity.

Ecumenical Movement

It is in the ecumenical movement that the different Christian confessions relate to one another today. The issue it deals with is how the different "universal" churches (composed of local churches) should be related.

As is well known, there has been a change, in both theory and practice, in the understanding of what these relationships should be and what purpose they serve. There is an awareness among the different confessions (except for some extremist Protestant sects and similar Catholic movements) that disunity is not willed by God, that it is an evil—whose origin is to be found in sin although it is not a sin to belong to one confession or another—and that it is a scandal. The evil of disunity is no longer attributed to a particular confession separated from the rest, but to disunity in itself. It is this disunity as such and the scandal it produces that must be overcome.

On the other hand, there is also recongition today that the diversity among the confessions with their different emphases regarding the understanding and practice of faith bears an aspect of mutual enrichment, inasmuch as historically and in practice some confessions have emphasized certain elements that are basic to faith, and other confessions have emphasized others. It is a diversity that is enriching both in principle and in what it has yielded in practice.

This new ecumenical attitude therefore presupposes that a confessionally-based sort of Manichaeism and mutual condemnation between confessions has been overcome; it assumes mutual respect and acceptance, and it especially assumes the urgent need for unity between the different confessions.

The point I want to develop is that the ecumenical movement will function better if the relationship between the different confessions is understood in terms of solidarity, "bearing with one another." This is simply an extension of the formal framework I have been using for this entire analysis. But what I wish to underline is that for such interconfessional solidarity to exist there must be an antecedent and underlying solidarity of each and every confession toward the poor. This is so for the general reasons already set forth and specifically because ecumenism is based on overcoming disunity and scandal. And the diverse confessions will not overcome them in a Christian manner if they do not overcome the basic disunity and scandal afflicting humankind itself. I therefore intend to reformulate the premises of ecumenism, with a view to understanding it as solidarity between confessions.

Interconfessional solidarity without a preliminary solidarity with the poor of this world is out of touch with reality, anti-Christian, and difficult to achieve in real history. I therefore want to analyze how the primary solidarity with the poor relativizes and unmasks certain assumptions of the ecumenical movement and at the same time provides premises for building ecumenism upon a firmer foundation.

Division

The ecumenical movement assumes that in itself division is something evil and not willed by God. But we must examine the seriousness of this evil and its varying degrees. If division means simply the existence of differences between confessions, that would not be an evil at all, and might even be enriching.

If division means the lack of unity in some formulations of the faith, in the liturgy, and in the way the church is organized, that might be an evil for a church that understands itself as "one"; but it would not in general be regarded as a grave defect. However, if division means noteworthy and opposed differences in the substance of the faith and practice of the gospel regarding God's will for the world of the poor, that division would be an evil inasmuch as it would simply reproduce among the diverse Christian confessions the basic division existing in humankind.

The division that is the most striking and scandalous is the division between the poor and the oppulent, between oppressed and oppressors. That division is not simply a lack of unity, and it is not simply the expression of the fact that the hoped-for unity of the human race awaited in the eschatological eon has not yet arrived. Rather, in itself it is sin, and fundamental sin. The fundamental division in humankind is that between life and death, between those who die because of oppression and those who live because of it.

It is on the basis of this fundamental division that the evil involved in other divisions must be judged, and it is on the basis of the urgency of overcoming this fundamental division that the urgency of attaining any other kind of unity must be judged, including the unity of Christian confessions. Confessional division would be fundamental if some were to stand on the side of oppression and others on the side of salvation. Fortunately, there is no such division that actually occurs. What I have in mind in making such a drastic description of what a fundamental division would be is to propose what the fundamental unity should be: conceiving and practicing a faith that stands in favor of life and not of death for human beings. This kind of unification around such a central point would unify the churches in an interconfessional way.

Scandal

The ecumenical movement assumes that division, in addition to being evil, is a scandal—that is, it seriously impedes the acceptance of the faith and entails loss of credibility for the churches vis-à-vis the world. But again we must recall what is the fundamental scandal the churches may give, so that we may better understand how much scandal there actually is in their division. In the New Testament the greatest scandal a Christian and believer can give the world is inconsistency between what is expressed as faith and the practice of that faith. Addressing Jewish believers, Paul says:

> Now then, teacher of others, are you failing to teach yourself? You who preach against stealing, do you steal? You who forbid adultery, do you commit adultery? You who abhor idols, do you rob temples? You who pride yourself on the law, do you dishonor God by breaking the law? [Rom. 2:21–23].

And Peter says to Christians:

> Among you also there will be false teachers who will smuggle in pernicious heresies. They will go so far as to deny the Master who acquired them for his own, thereby bringing on themselves swift disaster. Their lustful ways will lure many away [2 Pet. 2:1–2].

The effect of this inconsistency is described with words that could scarcely be more harsh: "Because of you God's name is blasphemed among the nations" [Rom. 2:24, *Bibl. Lat.*]. "The way of truth will be defamed" (2 Pet. 2:2, *Bibl. Lat.*).

For believers "blaspheming God's name" is undoubtedly the greatest scandal. And it takes place on the level of ethical conduct, of the practice of the faith at primary levels. Today the name of God is blasphemed—and unfortunately it does happen—when churches of any confession whatsoever ignore the problems of humankind, or relativize them in God's name or, worse yet, actually stand on the side of those who oppress the poor.

That is the point from which we must judge how great a scandal there is in disunity, and not the other way around. That is why a formulation of the ecumenical movement that, in the legitimate search for unity, would not seek at the same time to overcome the primary scandal and indeed give its overcoming a logical primacy would in itself be scandalous. It would also be scandalous to formulate the ecumenical movement in such a way that the topics it took up, the expectations it evoked, and the accomplishments it celebrated would ignore overcoming the fundamental scandal or treat it as something secondary. Such a course would not lead to a Christian way of achieving church unity. It is in the effort to overcome the fundamental scandal, in basic consistency with faith in God and a practice in accordance with that faith, that the churches will gradually unite—even though there remain differences in the way things are formulated.

These reflections point to a suspicion and an exigency. The *suspicion* is that down at the bottom of the ecumenical movement there lies a fundamental division that is not between confessions as such but between different ways of living the faith in a Christian and ecclesial manner, and that this division runs through the diverse confessions. It would follow that the unity sought and achieved on the level of the way the faith is formulated covers over a division that is real and profound, and that, on the other side, running through different formulations of faith there may be a fundamental unity in what is primary in faith.

The *exigency* is that the ecumenical movement must be relativized—for both theological and ecclesial reasons. Theological relativization means that the ultimate aim of the ecumenical movement ought to be the overcoming of the fundamental division in humankind, and that it is around this task that the work to overcome interconfessional differences ought to be carried out. Relativization in an ecclesial sense means that the boundary line today is not between different confessions, but that in fact it passes through them all. Before seeking unity of the churches we must therefore seek that truth of the church wherein the different confessions can be united.

Such a relativization would be quite fruitful for the ecumenical movement. Without it the movement toward church unity would be absolutized as something ultimate and definitive, and that would simply be proof of ecclesiastical concupiscence. However, when it seemingly forgets itself as it strives to provide the world with a way to solve *its* division, the church becomes truer to itself and lays down the true foundations for interconfessional unity, as indeed the experience of recent years has shown.

The ecumenical movement should not assume that the basic elements of faith are sufficiently assured in the different confessions and that the point now is to draw closer on relatively minor points of faith. Rather it should aim at tempering the foundations of faith in an interconfessional way: faith in a God of life, liberating and crucified; faith in Jesus as the one who announces the good news to the poor, denounces and unmasks the sin of the powerful, as the definitive servant of Yahweh, who shoulders the sin of the world and is executed by this sin, and is therefore raised up by the Father; a faith that is translated into the following of Jesus in the changing situations of history as it unfolds.

Seeking ecumenical unity through mechanisms that are purely ecumenical is not the answer. The answer must be sought in what can really make possible and set in motion a true unity. And that is nothing else but what I have called the foundations of faith.

Such a common basis for ecumenism has in fact led to a deep solidarity of different Christian confessions with the poor, at least in Latin America. Most of the poor in Latin America are Catholics. It would be a mistake to understand the ecumenical movement in Latin America as aid from Protestant confessions to Catholics. The wider and better view is that aid has come from different confessions to Christians who are poor.

This approach to the poor has unveiled the fundamental division in humankind and has automatically relativized division between the churches; it has posed the problem of unity in faith more from the side of faith than from the side of unity; it has emphasized as an essential ingredient in this faith the defense of the poor and the struggle for their liberation; it has clarified the essential elements of the faith that really come to be shared in common even though differences in formulation do not disappear. The result has been an important movement toward unification between the different confessions within Latin America, and also in the First World as its churches relate to Latin America. At the same time, other divisions have deepened, not between the confessions as such but within any church of any confession to the extent that its members have or have not entered into solidarity with the poor.

The different confessions have their own doctrines of faith and their own particular formulations. The poor question and challenge the reality of both. The poor present the different churches with an otherness that is greater than their mutual differences, and that is why they can be so challenging. But they also are the ones who make unification possible. The poor are a mediation of God in ongoing history, a mediation of the Lord who is present in those who are crucified, the ultimate criterion of the faith around which all the confessions must be united. The poor actually bring to pass what is called, because it is so difficult to achieve, the "miracle" of union; they are also mediators of God's captivating power. The unending prayer of the churches to God that the grace of unity be granted is to a great extent being answered through the paradoxical power of the poor, through the mysterious creativity that solidarity with them produces.

Unity in faith between different confessions may be described as a movement toward unity in faith that is set in motion and kept in motion by solidarity. The greater the solidarity of the confessions with the poor, the purer will be their faith and the truer it will be in practice. By the same token it will be a faith that is increasingly shared in common.

Within this movement of basic solidarity the ecumenical movement among the diverse confessions can itself be viewed as another instance of solidarity, as different confessions bearing with one another, each giving the best of its unique tradition and also receiving from the other confessions. Although the following summation is in no way an exhaustive or exact description, it is undeniable that the Catholic Church has emphasized the necessity of works for salvation, the importance of the sacraments as focal points where grace is conferred in history, the importance of tradition as a historical and ongoing mediation of God's revelation, a certain autonomy and substantivity to be found in nature. Protestant churches have emphasized the importance of personal faith, the gratuitous nature of salvation, the efficacy of the word. The Eastern churches have emphasized the importance of contemplation, the liturgy as celebration, and a view of salvation as affecting not only human history but the very cosmos.

This diversity of emphases that some years ago was often presented as reflecting basic opposition is now seen as mutually enriching. The ecumenical movement as conventionally understood has no doubt been a help. But I believe that the real synthesis of these varied emphases is being accomplished within grassroots solidarity with the poor. At least in Latin America this synthesis is taking place, even though it is not being done formally in order to achieve ecumenical unity. Word and sacrament, revelation in scripture and in the signs of the times, faith and works, prayer and justice, understanding of the present and reevaluation of church history, basic autonomy and trust in God—all these are different aspects that are being brought together in synthesis because that is what basic solidarity with the poor demands when that solidarity is worked out without any limits imposed a priori. In this way we find a model for understanding the ecumenical movement—a model at once formal and yet historical: solidarity between the different confessions, with each one contributing the best it has, and each advancing in faith, starting from the true foundations of that faith, and hence converging toward unity in faith, "bearing with one another in faith." All this is set in motion by basic solidarity with the poor.

Solidarity as Bearing with One Another in Faith

Our aim in the previous considerations has been to show how solidarity furnishes a model that enables the different churches or confessions to maintain, recover, enhance their identity in relation to other churches and confessions. What we now want to show is that solidarity may also be applied to the faith of believers—that is, that the personal act of faith, what is ultimate in each person, should be made with an openness to the personal faith of others. Thus "bearing with one another" reaches the realm of personal faith.

It is quite clear in Christian revelation that faith is the act of an individual person. It is an act by which the person stands before God to hear and receive God's self-manifestation, to respond to that manifestation with a total commitment, and in so doing to correspond fittingly to the reality of God. This act is deeply personal; there is no way to delegate to anyone else the responsibility for making it. That is why the scriptures often dramatize the "solitude" of the act of faith, as is shown prototypically in the faith of Abraham, who must leave his land and what he knows and enter the unknown; in the scene of the annunciation to Mary, whose only response is her fiat; in Jesus' prayer in the garden, where he is alone with God—the way the scene is set emphasizes this solitude—and accepts the will of the Father. There is something personal and nontransferable in the act of faith, and in this sense the "personalist" conception of faith is correct and continues to be valid.

Nevertheless, in the scriptures the act of faith in its personal and nontransferable dimension is often directed to the faith of others. Personal faith has a relationship to the faith of others. One expression of it is that of confirming others in the faith. Thus we read that those who are strong in faith "confirm" (Luke 22:32, *Bibl. Lat.*), "strengthen" (1 Thess. 3:2, *Bibl. Lat.* and "complete" (1 Thess. 3:10, *Bibl. Lat.*) the faith of others, and those who are weak in the faith can find help in the great witnesses of faith (Heb. 11) and especially in Jesus who lived faith in its originating and full sense (Heb. 12:2).

Another way of seeing the relatedness of faith, and one that is applicable on a wider scale, appears in Paul's words to the Romans, "For I long to see you . . . that we may be mutually encouraged by our common faith" (Rom. 1:11–12). What he is speaking of here is not a one-way help from the believer Paul, a teacher and moreover an apostle, to the faith of others who are presumed to need help. It is a two-way aid, a mutual giving and receiving of faith itself—in other words, bearing with one another in faith.

Being related to the faith of others is therefore inherent in personal faith. That is in fact what these New Testament passages show. What I should like to clarify is that this mutual— horizontal—relatedness to the faith of others is something essential and inherent just because the content of faith is nothing else but the mystery of God. Precisely because God is mystery, faith in the mystery of God must be related to the concrete faith of others in this mystery.

The mystery of God has been formulated in an authoritative way in revelation and in the magisterium of the church. For that purpose delimiting formulations have been employed. Thus it is stated that God is love, truth, omnipotence, absolute origin and future, grace and salvation, tenderness and mercy, precept and admonition, and so forth. Nevertheless, these formulations are not of such a nature that all believers will grasp them in an equal manner or degree. They are circumscribed formulations, and no one individual can grasp any of them exhaustively. They are different, though complementary, aspects, and no one person can grasp equally their different emphases. When these delimited truths are grasped in the concrete—and that is where faith takes place, and not simply in the cataloging of its contents—different elements in the concrete history of believers are at work: their personal situation, age, sex, culture, their own life story, their social and economic position, and so forth. These circumstances of their own history are both what make possible and what condition the way that the mystery of God is grasped differently and in differing degrees; they are what "concentrate" the comprehension of God's mystery in real circumstances, in real events, with the result that certain persons come to accent one or another aspect of this mystery. Although the mystery of God has been expressed formally in revelation, its being grasped in history nevertheless depends on the concrete way that the believer's own life unfolds.

The diversity of ways of "concentrating" the mystery of God is what actually makes it possible for us to keep God as mystery, beyond simply repeating in orthodox fashion that such is in fact the case. As there appear new ways in which the mystery is embodied, the mystery proves that it is indeed unmanipulable mystery; and these new aspects are what break with our natural tendency to think that in a particular embodiment we possess God. Moreover, the different embodiments sometimes emphasize aspects of God's mystery that seem irreconciliable in ongoing history: justice and mercy, liberation and peace, tenderness and imperation, and so forth. The mystery of God is "reduplicative" mystery.

The conclusion here is that, inasmuch as the content of the mystery of God is precisely "mystery," the faith of one person must be related to the faith of others. This is a way to preclude absolutizing one's own grasp of the mystery of God or trivializing the utopian aspect of its content. It is the practical way to retain the degree of not-knowing that must be part of any authentic knowledge of God. The "others" with their different embodiments of the mystery of God are those who enable one to avoid falling into the temptation of absolutizing one's own grasp and thus really trivializing the dimension of mystery in God. Those who would in principle refuse to open their own faith to the faith of others would be rejecting the mystery of God.

In a positive sense, we must be actively open to the faith of others if we are to continually grasp the mystery of God and allow it to be revealed in all its richness. In this way, with everyone taking part, we may ever more fully grasp the mystery of God. In a back-and-forth fashion, our conception of God comes ever closer to the reality.

The same thing must be said of faith as the real commitment of the human being to God. This commitment, as faith made real, cannot be delegated to anyone else. Theologically, what makes it possible is simply God's grace. That, however, does not mean that a person should not be oriented to the actual faith of other persons in the very process of making the commitment of faith. The real faith of other persons is, as it were, the way that the grace leading to one's own commitment is mediated within ongoing history.

The commitment of faith is described in formal terms as *total* commitment of the human person to God. But again this commitment has specific nuances that arise from the actual circumstances of the particular believer. Depending on these circumstances, the commitment of faith will be manifested as humbling oneself and kenosis, as the practice of love in its different forms (humanitarian aid, justice, pardon, marriage, friendship, and so forth), as the sacrifice of one's life—martyrdom.

It is through all these things that the commitment of faith is made, but as a result of differing situations sometimes one aspect will be emphasized over another. By way of example, believers who live in affluence will not emphasize prayer of petition so much, because one petitions when one does not have, whereas the poor will indeed petition in their prayer (and it does not necessarily indicate superstition or alienation). Poor believers, who have been kept down, will show their commitment precisely in their efforts for liberation, whereas believers who enjoy abundance will have to make a conscious effort to give up the trappings of their "superiority." Poor believers will be more ready to express gratitude and will demonstrate what it means to give out of poverty, whereas others will encounter radical demands on their generosity. Believers who find themselves in a conflict will go all the way to the point of martyrdom, whereas others will lend their support from outside to try to stop it. Believers who live in the Third World will manifest the simplicity and security of their faith, whereas what others offer will be their fidelity to the faith in a secularized world that is full of doubts and challenging questions.

Much more could be said about the concrete shape of each act of personal praxis that the act of faith implies. The point to emphasize is that the concrete reality of every believer's life at once conditions and yet makes possible the external act of personal response. The fact of being male or female, married or single, white-collar worker or blue-collar, for example, and the specific impact that they have on one's life, are major components of what shapes one's concrete reality. But what we most want to stress is that each believer's concrete personal commitment is something that challenges, stimulates, and opens possibilities for the commitment of others.

In this fashion, the very act of faith, which is personal and nontransferable, is made in solidarity with others; it lives from the faith of others. For example, a readiness to accept a lowering of one's own status or to be involved in the struggle for justice is certainly spurred by the real faith of poor Christians. On the other hand, the poor are remotivated in their own faith when they are supported by others. The prayer of

petition by the poor no doubt will help well-off Christians discover areas of impoverishment in their own personalities and
lives, and so they will turn to God through the prayer of petition. And active faith, the readiness to work and struggle, can
enrich the faith of those who have tended to concentrate on
petitionary prayer.

We could go on to list and analyze many other examples.
But what is most important is the conclusion: the faith of
others is important for one's own faith. In the de facto course
of events, it is essential, as has clearly been shown in Latin
America.

Insofar as it is the faith *of the other* it always challenges
one's own faith, and questions whether one's commitment is
enough or whether important aspects of commitment to God
have been left out. Insofar as it is the *faith* of the other—that
is, an embodiment of the miracle of faith—it is something
enabling and encouraging for one's own faith.

When all—or a significant group—express and embody
their own faith in connection with the faith of others, the
process of mutual giving and receiving takes place, and
through this mutual interchange there occurs what would be
total commitment to God if it reached the ideal and utopian
stage; in actual practice it never reaches it fully. To conceive
of personal commitment to God through faith within a
process of giving and receiving the faith of others is the practical way to avoid placing limits on the commitment of faith.
By not putting a priori limits we are again affirming that the
correlate of this commitment is the mystery of God.

All I have been saying may be summarized in the following
statement: it is the person who believes—but not in isolation.
The traditional way this idea has been expressed is that it is
the person who believes, but within the church; in a more
up-to-date form we could say that it is the person who believes, but within the people of God. In both cases, the
"within" is not just a spatial representation, nor is it meant to
suggest two instances of faith positioned side by side, as it
were, and logically independent of each other. Rather it signi-
fies an essential openness to others in order to give to them,

and receive from them, faith in its concrete form. In this sense, it could be said that we believe together and together we approach the mystery of God.

This statement should have a priori plausibility: there will be a better grasp of God's mystery and a better response to it when it is the whole of God's people, with the sum total of partial and complementary faiths, that approaches God.

Viewed a posteriori this in fact seems to be what has happened. To the degree that the people of God has been better established, faith has been made real, both as comprehension of the mystery of God and as commitment to that mystery. But what is important to realize—and here we end where we began—is that this people of God is being built up from the poor; and the "church" has become "people of God" in its solidarity with the poor. This solidarity is what has set in motion a process wherein the people of God and its faith is being built up.

Once we seriously understand that to be a human being is to be co-responsible with other human beings and especially with the poorest, that to be church is to be co-responsible with other churches, especially the most persecuted, we then understand that to be a believer is to be co-responsible in and with the faith of others, especially of the poorest. Solidarity in the faith is not a routine and empty formula; it brings out how faith is made real, a "bearing with one another" in the direction of the realm of faith.

Let us be mindful, however, that this solidarity in faith is not made real simply because one decides so with an act of will and in an idealist manner. This kind of solidarity, one that reaches the depths of faith, becomes real when it starts out from the human solidarity of bearing with one another on the primary levels of life where the death and life of human beings are at stake. This primary solidarity is not something optional for solidarity in faith, for in it is expressed what is new and scandalous in the Christian vision of history: a circular relationship between God and the poor. Puebla says the poor are "made in the image and likeness of God . . . to be his children [but] this image is dimmed and even defiled." Hence independently of their moral or personal condition, "God takes on their defense and loves them" (§1142). Because of this primordial circularity between God and the poor, any ecclesial solidarity in the faith must of necessity pass through solidarity with the poor. And contrariwise, when this occurs, there emerges the miracle—not likely to be achieved through other means—of churches bearing with one another, and Christians bearing with one another, in faith.

A Closing Word in Memory of Archbishop Romero

In all I have said, I have made a presentation of solidarity that is idealized but not idealist. It is idealized because we have not mentioned or examined the other side of the coin: unconcern for the poor, divisions within the church, new efforts in the church to return to imposition from the top. Nor have we examined how insufficient is the solidarity shown toward the gravely serious situation of the people and the church in El Salvador, Guatemala, or Haiti.

But this presentation is not idealist: I have based it on historical facts that are more than enough for elaborating a Christian theory of solidarity. To give just one example from the hundreds that could be cited, let me quote the words of an English Catholic. "I am a Catholic," he said. "I teach a religion class. And yet I find atheistic humanism attractive. But when I hear what Christians in El Salvador are doing and I recall the witness of Archbishop Romero, without exactly knowing why, I really feel like a Christian. My darkened faith becomes real again." This English Catholic is one of so many who support El Salvador from afar.

If I had to provide examples to make what I have said understandable, nothing could shed more light than would reflection on Archbishop Romero. He launched a massive process of solidarity and, once it was in motion, he knew how to live the reality of the church and his own faith in solidarity with others. I shall therefore close with some brief quotations that may illustrate everything that has been said here.

Archbishop Romero understood quite well that at the root of this process is the solidarity of the church with the poor and oppressed, and he stated it in an utterly radical way: "The church suffers the lot of the poor: persecution. Our church is proud that the blood of its priests, catechists, and communities has been mixed in with the massacres of the people, and that it has continually borne the mark of persecution" (Feb. 17, 1980).

He was extremely happy to see how this solidarity with the poor led to solidarity with the people and the church of El Salvador: "There are countless letters offering solidarity and encouragement for us to continue living out this witness" (Second Pastoral Letter, 1977). And he responded to it at the end of his life, a month and a half before being murdered, when solidarity had reached great proportions:

> I could find no better place and time than this opportunity so kindly offered by the University of Louvain, to say from the bottom of my heart: thank you! Many thanks, fellow bishops, priests, sisters, and lay persons, for so generously linking your lives, your strivings, your economic contribution to the concerns, works, weariness, and even persecutions we encounter in the fields of our pastoral work [Feb. 2, 1980].

He was also happy to see how ecumenical solidarity arose and grew: "We have received endorsements from many separated brothers and sisters, both inside and outside the country, and we wish to thank them publicly for their gesture of comradely and Christian concern" (Second Pastoral Letter, 1977). And he pointed to the root of true union:

> [It is the] hope of union, which is present in prayer now being made in all Catholic and Protestant churches that do not allow the gospel to be manipulated, who know that the gospel is not a toy of either politics or of particular interests, but that it must remain on a higher level and be capable of rejecting anything that muffles the true gospel message. Along with our Protestant brothers and sisters we will continue to seek a gospel that will be really at the service of our peoples, who have suffered so much [Jan. 21, 1979].

It is harder to document with quotes the impact the faith of others had on Archbishop Romero's personal faith. Because of his natural modesty he did not speak of what was deepest in him. But there is no doubt that contact with his people changed him also at the deepest levels and that from the poor of his people he gathered strength for his own faith and his own hope: "With this people, being a good pastor is not hard at all. It is a people that presses into service those of us who have been called to defend their rights and be their voice" (Nov. 18, 1979). "I believe the bishop always has a great deal to learn from the people. And it is in the charisms that the Spirit gives the people that the bishop finds the touchstone for his own authenticity" (Sept. 9, 1979).

Finally, Archbishop Romero saw that any solidarity relating to the church, ecumenical concerns, or even God must of necessity be rooted in the primary human solidarity—that with the poor. As he used to say, the suffering of the poor touches God's heart. "The church of my archdiocese has striven to incarnate itself in this world that lacks a human face, which is presently the sacrament of the suffering servant of Yahweh" (Feb. 2, 1980). "My position as pastor obliges me to stand in solidarity with everyone who suffers and to back every effort toward the dignity of human beings" (Jan. 7, 1979). Five days before he was murdered a reporter asked him what could be done for El Salvador and he answered, "Anyone who believes in prayer should realize that it is a power we need very much here and now. Anyone who believes in human fellowship should not forget that we are human beings and that persons are fleeing to the mountains, hiding there, and dying there" (March 19, 1980).

They "should not forget we are human beings." Perhaps there is no simpler or deeper way to describe the root of solidarity or to lay down firm foundations so that humanity may find full expression in the human race, Christianity be fulfilled in the churches, and the believer in God be fulfilled as a human being and a believer. When this "forgetfulness" is really overcome, the human being and the Christian believer are not alone; they are advancing along the road with others and the miracle we have described occurs: they bear with one another.

The Salvadoran church and people have helped many individuals and Christians not forget about the human being, and so they have grown in their humanity and their faith. Many have shown their gratitude to this church and this people for that reason. May what I have written also serve to express gratitude, along with Archbishop Romero, for the aid given to this people and the encouragement given to the faith of the Salvadoran church.

Juan Hernández Pico, S.J.

Solidarity with the Poor and the Unity of the Church

An Experience of Solidarity
with Archbishop Romero at Puebla

In February and March of 1979 I was the recipient of a special grace: being able to attend the ecclesial event known as the Third Conference of the Latin American Episcopate, at Puebla, Mexico. I attended somewhat on the fringe as one of a group of theologians and social scientists who met "outside the walls" of the Palafoxian Seminary in an effort to provide guidance and fraternal advice to a number of bishops who had asked us to be at Puebla, despite the fact that we had not been appointed as official conference experts. Some sisters near the seminary generously allowed us to use their convent for our work. Those bishops and other official conference participants came over to meet with us during noontime breaks and after finishing their work at night. In a climate of hope we talked over their concerns as the documents were being prepared. Archbishop Oscar Romero was one of those bishops and I was at Puebla because of his desire for such a theological dialogue. With him I shared an experience that may serve to introduce my thoughts on the underlying basis for the faith and hope that are involved in *solidarity with the self-liberative undertakings carried on by the peoples of Central*

43

America, which itself is a work of love. I should here like to recount this experience and reflect on it.

At the Puebla conference Archbishop Romero had a right to speak but not to vote, because he had been invited only as a member of the Pontifical Commission for Latin America. Throughout the whole conference he considered press interviews more important than sitting around a table drafting documents. What he wanted to do was to tell the world, from the privileged platform of Puebla, the story of Jesus as it was being re-created in the struggle and witness of his own Salvadoran church and people. This is the *first note* of the experience that his presence at Puebla afforded. For this leader and servant of his church and his people it was more critical to make known their crucifixion and their hope of attaining new life than to succeed in further polishing some expressions in official documents, although this kind of thing also concerned him, inasmuch as it involved a greater or lesser approximation to the truth that was his passionate concern.

The *second note* of the experience I am talking about came to light three days before the end of the conference. When the draft of the third version of the Puebla document had been handed to the participants for their consideration and vote and when our advisory work could therefore be considered finished, and it was clear that the rest was up to the Holy Spirit and to the clearsightedness and depth of feeling of those voting, our group invited the bishops who had asked us to come to Puebla over to have supper and meet for sharing and prayer, with love for the church. Some fifteen bishops managed to finish their other activities and showed up. With overflowing joy we celebrated two simple things: our humble work in the church, and fidelity to the hopes of the poor in our churches and our peoples.

The most beautiful moment came when Bishop Alano Pena, O.P., a Brazilian, asked what all of us could do for the persecuted and repressed peoples of Central America. The suggestion came immediately: write letters of solidarity and encouragement, which could be more explicit than the Puebla document about the suffering and hopes of the churches and peoples of Central America. These letters would be signed by the largest possible number of bishops and other conference participants. One would most certainly be sent to Archbishop Romero, to his local church, and to the Salvadoran people. Another, addressed to the president of the Episcopal Conference of Nicaragua, would recognize the suffering and also the dawning of hope in the Nicaraguan process of liberation, which at that point seemed half dead after the September 1978 antidictatorship insurrection had been put down with repression. Other letters were proposed.

Archbishop Romero stood up from the table. He could hardly speak as tears welled up in his eyes. With Christian gratitude he said that the trip to Puebla would have been worthwhile if it were only to receive this fruit of Christian solidarity. He sat down surrounded by a show of affection and Christian joy. We ended our session with an Our Father that we prayed as one of the greatest ecclesial experiences of grace in our whole lives. The letters sent to Archbishop Romero and to the president of the Episcopal Conference of Nicaragua, signed by more than forty Puebla participants, became impressive prophetic messages of the *kind of church unity that consists in bearing the burdens of building the kingdom of God from the perspective of announcing and putting into effect the good news that Jesus Christ announced to the poor.* In those letters fidelity to Jesus in the story of the poor was retold and it became Christian praxis in the church.

Other letters planned were in fact not written, because the bishops in question decided not to do so. Other peoples and other churches therefore did not receive this same prophetic sign of solidarity. This is not the place to analyze whether that decision was correct, but it seems an opportune occasion to examine the way that Archbishop Romero went about doing what he did.

The two notes that highlighted his public ministry—which for us meant the experience of being in the presence of a witness to Jesus Christ—were his central concern to tell the world how his church and his people were re-creating the story of Jesus, and his joy in receiving solidarity from other churches in their name. These two traits may be explained by studying the archbishop's pastoral experiences.

He was *close to Salvadorans as believers, as exploited, and as repressed,* close to them in the impulse of their faith and in the human dignity of their struggle. That closeness was the root of his activity at Puebla. It is well known that a considerable part of Oscar Romero's episcopal ministry consisted in keeping the doors of his chancery office wide open to let in all the suffering and all the hope of his people. Countless photographs bear witness to his recurrent presence in the poorest and most remote areas of his archdiocese, in order both to build up local churches and to build up personhood. His homilies are full of concrete references to his weekly visits there. The ongoing history of his people was something familiar—omnipresent—to him. It was not hard for him to find in his people the humanity of the poor—assaulted, despoiled, and left half dead in the middle of the road. It was not hard for him to recognize that upholding the repressed humanity of the poor was the main, and indeed only, Christian commandment.

The harsh fact was that *the Salvadoran Episcopal Conference was divided over how to interpret what was happening to the church and people of El Salvador.* Romero thus welcomed the joy of meeting other brothers in the universal episcopacy who showed solidarity with his vision and public ministry throughout his three years as archbishop of El Salvador. The gratitude he tearfully showed at Puebla was an ingrained habit with him. On the level of the universal church, he acknowledged God's graciousness in the gift of encouragement that came from his brother bishops. Their graciousness partly compensated for his unpleasant daily experiences within the episcopal conference of El Salvador.

As one who had taken Vatican II seriously, Archbishop Romero yearned to see put into practice the *co-responsibility and concern for all the churches* that the council had retrieved as part of the mission of bishops. That yearning enables us to understand his joy when he saw it beginning to be put into effect at Puebla. He recognized that this meant a step forward toward making church unity something real in history. He saw the unity of faith and of hope becoming concrete in the efficacious unity of love based on solidarity, a love that takes sides with those who are the objects of divine predilection, the poor of this earth.

Archbishop Romero's deep faith that the Spirit is present in developments within history is another clue to explaining his activity at Puebla. Although he was more conscious than many others of the ambiguity of any historical process, he nevertheless recognized that the cause of the poor as it was being pursued concretely by the popular organizations in El Salvador was where the Spirit was acting in history. He thought that solidarity with this cause was a favorable opportunity—a *kairos*—for retelling the story of Jesus in the midst of ongoing history, and so lending that story a Salvadoran youthfulness and contemporaneity.

That is why the concrete and committed solidarity he felt at Puebla made him so happy and grateful: out of the Christian roots of that solidarity he was able to show a *deep respect for the self-initiated undertakings of the poor in history.* This respect involved both the Christian hope of seeing their efforts head toward a new society that would show sacramental signs of parallelism with the kingdom of God, and an ever-watchful critique of ambiguities and deviations that could vitiate what the poor were undertaking in history. That is why he considered it important to support them in a Christian solidarity that recognized in their march forward hints of the coming of the kingdom. By the same token, he always kept in mind the human needs of the people—needs that were so often endangered.

I want to take this experience of Archbishop Romero and his reaction to solidarity as the starting point in this essay— and for a very simple reason. Long before becoming a theme in theological reflection, solidarity had been Christian praxis, a life of love based on faith and hope. It has been offered by Christian communities around the world, by men and women religious, by priests and bishops of a wide range of churches. This Christian praxis, especially (though not exclusively) among the poor, should be given theological elaboration, recognizing its consistency with the Spirit manifest both in the scriptures and in the fire that continually sets church communities and human history aflame.

Solidarity in the Bible: Hearing the Cry of the Poor and Responding to Their Undertakings in History

The goal of any Christian praxis is to incarnate the plenary goodness of the Father of Jesus Christ: "In a word, you must be made perfect as your heavenly Father is perfect" (Matt. 5:48). The Father's goodness, the Father's invincible fidelity to the cause of human beings, is confirmed in the struggle against all the evil of which human beings are capable and even against the abounding superhuman power of evil. In the Christian scriptures, in the tradition of the history of God with us, there is a prototype of the struggle that God's goodness and humankind wage against evil: the history of the exodus, the story of God's taking sides in the struggle between an oppressed people and its oppressor. Moreover, this prototype is to be found echoed in the recorded history of the life-and-death struggles of the poor as Israel took shape and in the initial following of Jesus.

Cry of the Poor: Evil Cannot Be Tolerated

The book of Exodus first describes how the Israelites came to Egypt and multiplied, and how the Egyptian empire saw in them a threat to its own survival. It then narrates the mechanism of oppression and repression the empire used to neutralize that threat: slavery, forced labor, genocide. It tells of the resistance the Israelites put up. According to exegetes, the Israelites were not yet a unified people but rather a tenuous grouping of foreign slaves whom Moses drew together under his leadership. "Yet the more they were oppressed, the more they multiplied and spread" (Exod. 1:12). The whole story is seen as a history of yearning for life, passion for life confronting a passion for death. What stands out is human suffering: "They made life bitter for them" (Exod. 1:13). On the other hand, when the historical tradition notes that some on the oppressor side show cooperation with the oppressed (the Egyptian midwives who do not obey the order of genocide), faith reads this as an act of taking sides on the part of a God who defends life (Exod. 1:17, 20–21).

In the context of this interpretation of history, what is seen as utterly intolerable is an attack on life, collective oppression—in a word, evil. It is utterly intolerable for human beings as well as for God. First for human beings: "A long time passed during which the king of Egypt died. Still the Israelites groaned and cried out because of their slavery" (Exod. 2:23). What is remarkable here is their refusal to accept being oppressed and having to live under domination. Something remarkable in collective consciousness is happening here: in the atmosphere of the ancient empires, where slavery was as socially acceptable as is hired labor today, a people rebels against slavery, murmuring cries of resistance and protest. It is a collective human cry, rejecting oppression and death as unjust and intolerable assaults on basic humanity. This cry comes from those "on the bottom," the powerless. It is important to note that Exodus does not say the Israelites complained *to God* or aimed their cry *at God*. Theirs was simply the cry of the struggle for life against the threat of death, not in a confrontation with nature, but in the confrontation that takes place in history between intolerable social conditions created or ratified by human beings and the determination of human freedom to change such conditions.

According to Exodus, God hears this cry even though it is not explicitly addressed to God: "As their cry for release went up to God, he hears their groaning and was mindful of his covenant" (Exod. 2:23–24). What stands out here is the enmity between God and oppression and God's closeness to the oppressed, God's taking sides in this confrontation within history. For Yahweh, whom Jesus of Nazareth will recognize as his Father with an intimacy and exclusiveness unprecedented in the Israelite tradition, it is intolerable that life be hemmed in with the injustice of oppression and repression that even go as far as genocide: this is unacceptable to the God of life, who is just to all, but who favors the victims when the human and social reality of oppression makes its appearance in history.

This image of God is so universal in the Christian scriptures that the "cry" of the oppressed becomes a technical linguistic term meaning an appeal reaching up to and moving God in unyielding fidelity to humankind. When Israel reflects theologically on the origins of evil in the world, the breakup of fellowship that this evil represents is imaged as the cry of the murdered brother's blood reaching up to God (Gen. 4:10). In the prophetic tradition it is said that God does not hear the prayer of those who have "their hands . . . full of blood" (Isa. 1:17–18), although God will enter into dialogue with those who "cease doing evil [and] learn to do good"—that is, of those who "make justice [their] . . . aim" and "redress the wronged." In the psalms the theme of God who defends the blood spilt when fellowship is broken and the theme of the cry of the oppressed are joined: "For the avenger of blood has remembered; he has not forgotten the cry of the afflicted" (Ps. 9:13). This same psalm reminds us that it is God's faithfulness to this cry that guarantees the final vindication of the hope that is part of the protest against injustice: "For the needy shall not always be forgotten, nor shall the hope of the afflicted forever perish" (v. 19). Those who pillage others, trying to cover over their oppression with rationalizing ideologies, will have to face God's resistance: " 'Because they rob the afflicted, and the needy sigh, now will I arise,' says the Lord; 'I will grant safety to him who longs for it' " (Ps. 12:6).

It is these two converging experiences—the experience of the intolerability of oppression and genocidal repression seeking to maintain injustice, and the experience of the God of Jesus Christ in the struggle against this death-dealing power—that today *resound in the reality what is taking place in Central America*. Oppressed and believing peoples—the people in El Salvador, the people of Guatemala, the people in Nicaragua—raise their cry and denounce the utterly intolerable evil of injustice and the genocidal repression unleashed against their struggle and their hopes. The Christian and ecclesial solidarity that hears this cry is an effort to be faithful by trying to hear as does the Father of Jesus Christ, and by emulating the divine goodness that takes sides. What is at stake here is the fidelity of the church to the God of Jesus

Christ. What is at stake is whether what the Latin American bishops pointed out at Puebla will become concrete in history:

> From the depths of the countries that make up Latin America a cry is rising to heaven, growing louder and more alarming all the time. It is the cry of a suffering people who demand justice, freedom, and respect for the basic rights of human beings and peoples.
>
> The cry might well have seemed muted back then [Medellín, 1968]. Today it is loud and clear, increasing in volume and intensity, and at times full of menace [Puebla documents, nos. 87, 89, in John Eagleson and Philip Scharper, eds., *Puebla and Beyond: Documentation and Commentary,* Maryknoll, N.Y., Orbis, 1979, p. 134].

The Liberative Programs of the Poor in History: Horizon of Human Goodness

It is clear that it was the particular attributes ascribed to God by Yahwistic faith (which is not necessarily the product of an archaic culture) that led the biblical writers to emphasize in an almost absolute manner the role of God as protagonist in the events that liberated the Israelites from oppression in Egypt—that is, in the day-to-day working out of the historical undertaking that transcended the years of slavery in Egypt. Nevertheless, we have already seen how the faith of Israel also understands God's breaking into history as a response to the mighty cry of the oppressed, which is both lament and protest, both being elements of resistance. Israel believes that this same movement within history of a group of slaves to resist oppression, which is extremely crucial for its beginnings as a people, has been taken up by God, who raised up a leader for the people and accompanied it in its epic quest for liberation.

In Israelite History and Prophecy. In the book of Joshua and in Judges and in parts of the books of Samuel the historical memory of Israel has left us traces of what it sought to build in the land of Canaan that it had occupied and recovered. I say "occupied" and "recovered" because today it is the well-founded opinion of many scripture scholars that the original grouping of persons that was to become the future Israel was peopled not only by emigrants who took part in the epic events of liberation from Egypt but also by those who inhabited Canaan: peasants from the mountains, wandering shepherds, fugitives from a quasi-feudal system who had become mercenaries—all of them stimulated by the arrival in Canaan of those who had been liberated from Egypt. Studies of the situation of the Middle East at that time show Canaan as a region organized into city-states dependent in a quasi-feudal manner on the Egyptian empire. The city-states in turn dominated the surrounding plains and mountains and forced their inhabitants to pay tribute. When the emigrants from Egypt burst into this region, with their experience of rebellion and liberation and their faith in Yahweh the God who oriented human beings toward freedom and egalitarian justice, it was probably the decisive stimulus that rekindled among those doubly dominated groups the hope for release from the oppressive Canaanite city-states. It was precisely this impetus of liberation, the legacy of those who had been slaves in the Egyptian empire, and the recurring rebelliousness of the inhabitants of Canaan (when both elements were joined in a viable historical project) that was understood in Israel's faith both as a revolutionary irruption into history and as a call from Yahweh to build something radically new in history.

Even in those texts where God's seemingly exclusive and all-absorbing role as protagonist stands out most, it is nevertheless quite plain that the background is the free initiative in history of the people made up of the exploited and oppressed. We find in the book of Joshua (1:1–18, esp. vv. 6, 7, 9, and 18) an example that is especially telling because there is an exact parallel in language. Scholars believe this whole first chapter is a product of Deuteronomist editors—that is, that it was produced during the Israelite exile in Babylon (after 586 B.C.) and it sought to reinterpret the history of the people as the consequence of its infidelity to the covenant. The Deuteronomist editors produce moral-theological texts taking a markedly stylizing approach to the underlying history. God here appears as the one who issues the command to march and occupy the land (v. 2), as the one who will give the land (v. 4), as the one who will put down any resistance on the part of the present inhabitants (v. 5), as the one who gives value to the work of carrying out the historical project (v. 6). Three times God exhorts Joshua to arm himself with courage: "Be firm and steadfast" (vv. 6, 7, and 9). Joshua transmits to the others the command to march. But they also respond to this command to begin the struggle using the same words ("Be firm and steadfast"), thus enabling us to see that as things actually happened it was not only God but also the people who encouraged Joshua to initiate a liberative projection into the future.

Furthermore, in the same chapter there survive deeply human traits that reflect the same reality in history—that is, a self-projection into history that an oppressed people in its consciousness experiences as its task and responsibility, although it is true that, in its faith, it also experiences it as God's undertaking. For example, the fact that the people and its leader are exhorted to courage is a reflection of the magnitude of the task entailed in building a society that is just and egalitarian, made up primarily of free federated peasants in the midst of a world where imperial and city-state forms of government predominate and lead to exploitation, injustice, and an inequitably stratified society. Joshua has the foresight to store up food for this difficult endeavor so that the rebels will not be defeated through hunger (v. 11), and he tells the men to arm themselves heavily to face the enemy (v. 14). Lying beneath the proclamation of Yahweh as protagonist, the historical memory retains clear traces of the historical projection as a human responsibility with the people as protagonist.

The first chapter of the book of Judges also retains historical recollections of how different groups, identified as "tribes" or segments of tribes confederated into Israel, over a period of time and with varying success carried out the occupation or reoccupation of the land of Canaan. The

Deuteronomists' concern is to show all of Israel united in the endeavor to occupy the land, and this concern is particularly clear in the first twelve chapters of the book of Joshua. This intention leads the editors to simplify and compress a complicated history. Nevertheless they do not go so far as to completely lose sight of the historical memories of the different struggles waged by many different components of the people so that Israel might be constituted an antistatist confederation, striving to reestablish a tribal solidarity of free rural landworkers.

This concern derives from a desire to impose retroactively on the past—as something normative for the formation of Israel "from the beginning"—the unity of worship in one place characteristic of the religious reform of King Josiah, which the Deuteronomists consider the ideal for Israel.

It is in songs like that of Deborah (Judges 5:1-31), a canticle of victory in war, that we can appreciate the historical undertaking of those who struggle to do away with exploitation, to overturn the domination of having to pay tribute, and to set up a new society that will be just and egalitarian. It is in canticles like this that we can get a glimpse of the kind of enemies the newly created Israelite confederation is struggling against. The enemy is not a whole people already occupying Canaan, nor is it ethnic groups different from those making up Israel; it is rather "kings," "princes" (v. 3), hostile military expeditions (v. 6), "warriors" and "the mighty" (v. 13), "horses" and "chariots," and finally the "kings of Canaan" (v. 19), one of whom is mentioned by name, Sisera (vv. 26, 28, 30). Hence they are dynastic sovereigns of the city-states of Canaan, with their system of exploitive domination and with their superior military technology. The song celebrates the victory of the Israelite peasantry ("the victories of the peasants of Israel" v. 11)—that is, of those rural landworkers who previously paid tribute in the system of exploitive domination maintained by the cities over the countryside. It celebrates the triumph of an army of free citizens who have answered the call to arms from among the different tribes in the Israelite confederation. There is rejoicing because the ambush tactics of this militia that knows the terrain have been successful against the powerful military expeditions organized by the coalition of local kings of the city-states, and the winners are now dividing up the conquered booty (vv. 6–7).

By putting this text alongside others from the same period that speak of the Israelite institution of "anathema" (that is, of the religious obligation to destroy enemies and share the booty), we can get a glimpse into that history and recognize that such a booty was not considered to be "stealing" but a collective "recovery" of the fruits of previously exploited labor, and that, moreover it did not go primarily to the Israelite leaders but was shared equitably among the people, as well as among the Levites, a priestly group in Israel that had no land of its own and did not follow the pattern of taking excessive taxes for worship, as was common in the systems of the surrounding peoples (see Josh. 8:27; 11:19; Num. 31:25–54; 1 Sam. 30:21–31).

The texts themselves show that it was the people who designated portions of those booties to the leaders who were its guides in the liberation campaign. The song of Deborah curses the "governors" of a city (Meroz) who had probably made a pact with the Israelite confederation and then not answered the call to arms (v. 23). And there is concern about those tribes of the confederation that did not participate in the common struggle of all Israel (vv. 17–18), but there is exaltation over those tribes who formed part of the "volunteers of Israel" in this battle (vv. 9 and 14–16)—that is, of those "volunteers of the people" who responded to the pact with a resolute willingness to defend the confederation no matter which members were under attack from the previous dominators, now defeated.

This same kind of memories can be read in the canticle of Miriam (later attributed to Miriam and Moses; Exod. 15:1–21) and in the canticle of Ana, the mother of Samuel (1 Sam. 2:1–19), so many themes of which later passed into Mary's canticle of victory, the Magnificat. It is in these canticles that the historical projection of a new society that Israel has set for itself is also seen as Yahweh's undertaking, as the horizon of justice that the God of Israel assimilates and calls others to.

Yahweh is so identified with this march forward of the oppressed in history that in Deborah's canticle the curse on those who did not go into battle falls on them because they "come not . . . to the help of the Lord" (v. 23, *Bibl. Lat.*), "victories of the peasants of Israel" are experienced as "victories of the Lord" (v. 11 *Bibl. Lat.)* in this faith that penetrates history.

Decades after the period reflected in the canticle of Deborah, the new element in history represented by Israel as a society of free landworkers confederated and held together by structures designed to guarantee justice to all, although surrounded by empires and city-states based on exploitive domination, is critically threatened again by military groupings settled in the coastal cities of Canaan and known in the Bible as the Philistines. Here also Israel's faith interprets the struggle between opposed historical forces as a struggle over fidelity to two irreconcilable experiences of God.

The monarchy to which Israel ultimately feels it must have recourse (with mixed feelings, because it represents a profound change in the course of its history—see Judg. 9:8–15 and 1 Sam. 8) is also experienced in faith as an enterprise in history that Yahweh blesses, insofar as it is viewed as the only way to avoid falling into slavery and exploitation. Israel is convinced that only a kind of national formation with greater cohesiveness than that of the tribal confederation can preserve the freedom and justice for which it struggled as a confederation. It is this historical projection—ambiguous because it risks easing Israel into slavery and internal injustice—that faith in Yahweh nevertheless interprets as the only horizon of freedom and justice humanly feasible, and so it seeks to channel its efforts toward that goal. For a period during the Davidic monarchy that healthy tension is maintained; later on the monarchy becomes increasingly tyrannical and (with some exceptions) the institution of the monarchy increasingly modifies the meaning of faith in Yahweh as one who acts in favor of the people and *through the people,* changing it to faith in Yahweh as acting in history in favor of the people but *through the king.*

The true prophets of Israel make a prophetic denunciation of the slavery and injustice that the deterioration of this faith into a rationalizing ideology increasingly causes, both in worship and in the social privileges of the courtly and military strata and subservient prophets. True prophets continue to keep alive the ideal of a historical march forward toward freedom and justice worthy of Yahweh. The magnetic attraction of what the poor of Israel wanted to achieve in history together with Yahweh is not lost either in exile, when that historical march forward has been stopped, or in the restoration (see Esdras and Nehemiah), or when national independence has been lost completely (see 1 and 2 Macc.).

In Jesus of Nazareth. The Israelite quest for freedom and justice, and its congruence with Yahweh's will and design, take on new meaning in Jesus of Nazareth. In a manner that is utterly unique Jesus acclaims Yahweh as his Father and at the same time as God of his people and of humankind—and especially as God of the poor. The meals Jesus shares with all the outcast, with those on the fringes of society and the oppressed in Israel, his claim that God's fatherhood applies especially to the poor as a sign that God rejects the negation of fellowship present when injustice and inequality prevail—all these are undeniable elements of the pattern of life and work of Jesus, a lifework of announcing and making real the kingdom of God.

In two complementary passages of John's Gospel this pattern is concentrated in a remarkable way: the anointing at Bethany (John 12:1–8) and the foot washing (13:1–20). The anointing at Bethany, put close to the gift of life, the rescue of life from death effectively shown in Jesus' raising of Lazarus, points to a Christian celebration of Jesus as font of life. In this anointing there is a strong echo of the eucharist, Jesus' last supper: "there [Bethany] a supper was given in his honor" (12:2, NEB). This is the only place in John's Gospel where the word "supper" appears, apart from those occasions where the reference is to Jesus' last supper. What is evoked, therefore, is not only the life that Jesus gives through his victory over death in the "signs" of power involving others (e.g., Lazarus) but also the life that Jesus gives through his victory over death in the trust with which he surrenders his own life for others and for the kingdom.

In this banquet of celebration what is affirmed is Jesus arisen as the personal force of life present forever in the community, even after his death, through the Spirit who will guide the personal and social history of his disciples and of humankind, both along the line of Jesus, "arousing memory of him," the memory of his praxis and his word (John 14:25–26), and for his cause ("he will bear witness to my cause"—John 15:26, *Bibl. Lat.*). But in the Christian celebration of life Jesus as a real presence within history, as a presence with a human face, will cease being the one who most immediately challenges his disciples and his people (the "church"). It will be *the poor* who will henceforth assume the human presence of Jesus and the challenge in his countenance. A way of relating to them that is not merely one of compassion because of their needs but an acceptance of them as members of the community with full rights—as persons whom the community takes on in an absolute form ("the poor you always have *with you*"—12:8—is the touchstone of the new community that celebrates the font of life—Jesus. Giving in to the power of money or making use of the poor— attitudes shown by Judas in the passage on the anointing (12:4–6)—can end only in wealth that is all-absorbing and in the domination of some human beings over others. The only way to be identified with Jesus and to respond to his challenge present in the face of the poor (Matt. 25:40) is to recognize the dignity of the poor and defend their cause even by giving one's life for them.

It is in the foot washing that the evangelist perceives the ultimate justification for an attitude of celebrating life in the name of Jesus and his continued presence in history through the Spirit, an attitude that motivates a table fellowship with the poor. There Jesus, the Lord, with the solemnity of someone making a final testament, fully lucid in the face of his oncoming death, completely assumes the mission of being servant of the community, the new people of God. He does so not as an act of humility in the sense of "modesty," but as one who is affirming that in the "new" human community there is no inequality in the sense of stratified ranks, nor is there any servitude, but only mutual service, a co-responsibility of brothers and sisters one to another, a friendship linked to the same mission and the same destiny (John 15:11, 14–15, and 20:17).

Jesus shows that he is "Lord" over the community and over humankind in a new way: by being first in service, making the disciples, and especially the poor, his equals and granting them the freedom of the children of God. In the evangelist's theological vision this sense of Jesus' action of service is found clearly in the sign that he and his disciples eat the last supper not as a commemoration of the passover in Egypt— that is, they do not eat standing up as "slaves" who await their liberation, but as "reclining" in the posture of a meal taken among free equals. His charge that they love one another, the soul of this freedom, will constitute the expression and following of this "love and fidelity," of this "love to the end" that Jesus incarnates as the revelation of God's "glory," and as the true image of God in God's basic attitude toward humankind (John 1:14, 18, and 13:1).

The historical reality that underlies this theological vision and provides a basis for the hope of the Christian community is the unending struggle waged by Jesus of Nazareth against "the enemy" (his expelling of "demons") and his denunciation of all those who have as their "father" the enemy of justice and freedom among human beings, the "father of lies" and a "murderer from the beginning" (John 8:43–44). The true nature of God, by contrast, was revealed from the beginning when Yahweh, the Father of Jesus, granted lordship over the earth to human beings, who were called to equality, freedom, and justice (Gen. 1 and 2), and by demanding that there be a sincere co-responsibility among human beings in a manner befitting sisters and brothers (Gen. 4).

In the Early Church. The apostles and the early Christian communities take on Jesus' liberative mission in history: they see it as destined to be the ferment of any historical undertaking that is just ("you are the salt of the earth"—Matt. 5:13) and as the answer to the yearning for wholeness found in any sincere attempt to help others (Luke 9:49–50). It is this purposefulness carried forward in the name of Jesus of Nazareth that forces them to resist all powers that try to suppress the connection between Jesus of Nazareth and any course of action showing signs of the kingdom of God (e.g., the dignity and reintegration into the community effected through the health that Peter restores to the man who was "crippled from birth"—that is, to someone who was segregated from Israel. "Judge for yourselves whether it is right in God's sight for us to obey you rather than God" (Acts 4:19). The New Testament, accordingly, teaches faith in a God who is faithful and favorable to undertakings creative of dignity, freedom, and justice—undertakings that can be incorporated into liberative projects that point toward the horizon constituted by the justice of the kingdom of God.

In Central America Today. In Central America today there are historical undertakings that the poor as a people have designed and embraced. In Guatemala, in El Salvador, and especially in Nicaragua, these self-projections have taken on a concrete shape; they crystalize the hope of the poor and their cause. Solidarity with these projects is a way of making real the Christian obligation to serve others, striving to draw on the legacy of Jesus and Israel in order to create conditions of equality, freedom, and justice among human beings. The church in Latin America has found it impossible to sidestep fidelity to this legacy. The preferential option for the poor, solemnly declared at Puebla, was translated into words of commitment in the bishops' Message to the Peoples of Latin America. The bishops invited all, "regardless of class, to accept and take up the cause of the poor as if they were accepting and taking up their own cause, the cause of Christ himself."

It is obvious that for those whose class position is structurally contradictory to the cause of the poor, this invitation is a call to conversion. It implies a real shift toward the popular classes in our countries and toward defending their interests as expressed in their own self-liberation efforts. The bishops' message makes this point quite clearly when it points to the socio-political reality where this conversion of the heart must be embodied structurally: "we believe that the reexamination and revision of [popular] religious and moral behavior should be reflected in the political and economic processes of our countries." What this means is that an approach that only alleviates the injustice of the system that creates poverty is not enough; solidarity involves taking on the *cause* of the poor and not only their *lot.*

For Christians, therefore, *the conflictive reality in history of a struggle between good and evil, between justice and injustice, being waged by the poor in our countries* (and by those who have taken on their cause despite their own class origins) *is a* locus theologicus *where God is breaking into history.* The Spirit is breathing there and keeping the memory of Jesus and his cause present. In the cause of the poor and the concrete way their struggles are actually waged, Christians are faced with a sign that is pregnant with meaning for the kingdom of God and they must accept and interpret that sign; notwithstanding all their ambiguity, the organized movements of the poor are indispensable, both at the level of leadership and at the level of structuration, if the poor are to achieve victory. And Christian solidarity is an indispensable response, one demanded by mutual service in love for this horizon of justice and freedom. The response of solidarity must be given in order to create a confluence between the opportune moment of grace *(kairos)* and the human endeavor in history, so as to be able to withstand the avalanche of injustice that seeks to prevent any such confluence.

Christian Solidarity: Humbly at Work within Human Solidarity

As concretely embodied, Christian solidarity with the cause of the Central American poor in their self-liberation efforts does not differ in its basic structure from solidarity that does not understand itself as based on faith in the God of Jesus Christ and love for him and his utter and absolute fidelity to the hope of the poor. Those who do not believe and yet take on this ultimate solidarity with the Guatemalan, Salvadoran, and Nicaraguan poor in their historical self-projections into a better future—and I highlight this point because at present it is a striking sign to the whole world—do so because these self-liberation projections are within reason, they are morally just, and they promise to open paths for the human race at large. Furthermore, when nonbelievers assume this solidarity they are repudiating daily torture and murder and "state terrorism" in the cases of Guatemala and El Salvador, and the terroristic arrogance of the United States government in its effort to forcibly impose the limits of its own tolerance on the new society that the people of Nicaragua are striving to build. That repudiation is translated into resistance and concrete struggles such as diplomatic initiatives, mediation proposals, forums for analysis and for restoring balance by presenting information objectively, protest marches, and the like.

All such actions *in their material reality in ongoing history* are not different from the rebellion that forms the material basis of the exodus narratives, or from the rebellion of the oppressed inhabitants of Canaan and their efforts to make alliances with other groups or to neutralize the surrounding city-states. Nor are they different from courses of action to deal with the hunger of the crowds, or social segregation, or illness both as physical suffering and social stigma, or to deal with the commercialization of religion or any other religious oppression—kinds of action that make up the de facto material reality of the signs performed by Jesus of Nazareth.

At this level of material reality in history and all the uncertainty it entails (human suffering continues to exist after Jesus' deeds as well as after structural change today), the difference in these actions is to be found in the different way they fit into different needs arising out of different situations in history, and from a different kind of awareness of how those needs should be dealt with. It is important to understand how differences of awareness and motivation can enter into the concrete expression of solidarity.

At this point it is important to emphasize that liberative projects undertaken in behalf of the poor—those that defend their interests, take on their cause, and try to find viable channels for them within the possibilities allowed by particular political contexts—are what Christian solidarity supports simply because they are what *human* solidarity supports. Any obligation of solidarity on the part of Christians does *not* arise because the project is defined as a Christian venture or a project of Christians. Obligation arises because the project is understood as human and humanizing; it does not need any supplemental religious legitimation above and beyond its inherent legitimacy.

Our faith as Christians helps us see both the *ultimate meaning* and the *sacramental character* of such projects: both in continuity and discontinuity with the kingdom of God, they lead toward it, and they offer glimpses of it in both practice and expression. We believe this because we believe that Jesus Christ is the seed sown in the whole world and in all human activity: "the Word [that became flesh in Jesus] contained life and that life was the light of human beings" (John 1:14, *Bibl. Lat.*). Therefore we believe that the Word, as God's self-projection and in perfect alignment with God's self-projection, embodied in creation and in Jesus of Nazareth, is inscribed in the destiny of humankind and its world as a force for life. Hence where there is a thrust for life and a human struggle for that thrust, our faith tells us that the force of life in Jesus Christ is at work. Both this and its opposite are expressly stated in the gospel:

> Everyone who practices evil
> hates the light;
> he does not come near it
> for fear his deeds will be exposed.
> But he who acts in truth
> comes into the light,
> to make clear
> that his deeds are done in God [John 3:20–21].

Hating the light means hating *the evidence of human goodness self-evident in life itself*. Hence, to commit evil is to act with no commitment, theoretical or practical, to the life of humankind and the life of the poor which is the acid test of the will for life for humankind. But one who acts in truth—

that is, with an enduring and irrevocable love for the life of humankind and especially for the life of the poor—is not putting into practice ideologies that mask things, but is acting with unshakable conviction and sincerity. Of such persons—whether or not they are graced with the gift of faith in Jesus Christ, the ultimate source of their inspiration—our faith tells us that what they intend and practice is "carried out in union with God." It should be absolutely clear that the force impelling them to solidarity is the attraction of human goodness that human beings who know how to love find in life itself and in the struggle for life, prior to all the meaning that our faith gives to life and the struggle for life—and to solidarity with both.

The self-liberation projects of the Guatemalan, Salvadoran, and Nicaraguan poor are taking place at *a particular point in history*. At any moment in history opportunities for life and for death can be proposed and readied. One important aspect of human responsibility lies in calculating those opportunities. For Central America the period of the 1970s was marked by the intensification of exploitive and oppressive governmental measures within our countries—measures that flatly contradicted the proposals for development and the ideologies of freedom, participation, and justice that had been spread so widely as values and goals. A consequence has been the awakening of the consciousness of the poor in Central America. They then took the first step out of the fatalism with which they traditionally regarded misery and weakness. They have then moved on to resistance, even though it was at first sometimes embodied only as a cry of complaint and protest.

In addition, the power center of the dominant world system, the United States of America (and its own most powerful classes), had been losing hegemony within that system. For years it tried to reestablish that hegemony with the Vietnam war in Southeast Asia, and then through trilateral alliances with Western Europe and Japan, and by making the world tripartite, with the United States, the Soviet Union, and the People's Republic of China balanced off. In the interval, groups leading the cause of the poor in Central America perceived the loss of hegemony by their powerful northern neighbor and its relative neglect of its "police" activity in the area as signaling the emergence of an opportunity that could be put to advantage.

The Meaning of Solidarity

Solidarity with the liberating projects of the Central American poor means first of all adopting a correct vision of the opportunities for life that the poor of Central America have at this particular period in history. It means adopting a correct vision in co-responsibility with the movements that are heading this struggle for life, intelligently using the opportunities this period affords. It means adopting such a vision in co-responsibility with those who put their very lives at stake in what they are doing. Such solidarity also means co-responsibility with others who rally around this view of contemporary history. New forces for national unity spring up, and Central Americans begin to revise their pessimistic attitude toward their homeland, seeing it now as a land that is fruitful and life-engendering.

It is obvious that there is nothing in all this to prevent Christian faith from moving beyond merely acknowledging the legitimacy of making good use of this specific period in history in favor of the poor, and in addition seeing in this period of history a *kairos*, a time of grace for humankind—grace that is both dynamic and structural, offered as a gift and as a task for human co-responsibility toward brothers and sisters who are poor.

The basic reason for exercising the responsibility of taking advantage of this period co-responsibly with the organized movements of the poor in Central America is *the fact that the dire poverty of these peoples is intolerable and the struggle to rescue them from that poverty is something that is self-evidently good.* Monopoly over land, both rural and urban, in our countries is one of the basic roots of the hunger, the widespread malnutrition, the high infant mortality, the work that squeezes the last drop of vitality out of laborers, the chronic unemployment and underemployment—in a word, the slow death suffered by most Central Americans.

To show a practical concern for rescuing the poor of Central America from this misery, to do so in solidarity with those poor and their organized movements (which are the only ones that have shown they actually intend to do so), *is what solidarity means at this moment*. This is a concrete translation of "binding the wounds" of the man who was assaulted, beaten, and left on the road half dead (Luke 10:30—35). This is a contemporary version of "feeding the hungry and giving the thirsty something to drink" (Matthew 25:35-36). Such is the case not because the gospel says so; rather, the gospel says so because this is how things are.

When others support programs for a government with a popular base, as proposed by the movements of the poor in Central America, when they show concern over intolerable deprivation and unjustly inflicted misery, when they seek to aid the uprooted and refugees, when they support projects and activities that aim at rescuing persons from that situation and laying the groundwork that will make it possible for natural resources and life to be shared justly, such solidarity is what makes the difference between life and death for the poor of Central America.

It is obvious that above and beyond the goodness inherent in efforts to relieve hunger and thirst, as well as in efforts to provide structures to eliminate malnutrition, Christian faith sees the countenance of Jesus, who is today a victim of hunger or thirst, or on his way to vanquishing them, the face of Jesus in the desperately poor of Central America and in the overall lines of their struggle for life.

Where Solidarity Should Begin

The fact that the poor of Central America, the masses of rural and urban laborers, are weak, the fact that they have been kept from playing an active role in the history of their countries, as evidenced in repeated fraud when they vote, in a constitutional provision (in El Salvador) prohibiting rural workers from unionizing, and a provision (in Guatemala) making it illegal to strike during the harvest season for export products, and finally the fact of the implacable repression of any just effort toward solutions that would allow the people to participate in politics—all these are elements that form part of the starting point for the kind of responsibility implied in solidarity with the peoples of Central America today.

The violation of a people's desire to share in the shaping of its own history means denying the humanness of the majority of the population, refusing them a share in the human condition. Awareness of this human condition makes that violation today ethically intolerable. The classes that have been excluded from history have struggled so that their voice may be heard and they may play a role in the making of history. They have endured attacks on their lives, their bodies, and their spirit, by torture and mass murder, whenever they have sought to put an end to their exclusion. That struggle has in itself a self-evident goodness that does not need to seek legitimation from any external source. This does not mean that Christian faith may not view such a struggle as a legitimate path for achieving *in the Spirit* the happiness that is promised to the poor: that they will possess the earth and will overcome every oppressive institution that tries to withhold from the human community and especially from the poor the potential for shaping this earth so as to satisfy the true needs of all.

Among the elements that constitute a starting point for a response of solidarity with the movements of the Central American poor, perhaps one of the most intolerable in a human sense is *the effort to misrepresent their humanity as they struggle to take an active role in history and share the earth in a more equitable fashion*. The mass media are used to spread around the world an image of "terrorism" applied to the resistance with which the poor try to gain respect for their humanity and their right to attempt self-liberation. The hypocrisy with which some observers denounce the suppression of the Solidarity movement in Poland, while supporting and defending repression of the struggles of the poor in Central America, is in itself so evil that no condemnation adds anything more, even when it comes from faith or some ideology.

The ancient Amarna letters, documents written by the quasi-feudal rulers of Canaan to the Egyptian pharaohs about a century before the foundation of Israel, already attest to the incipient rebellion of the inhabitants of Canaan against the dominant system. In those documents the rebels are always called *hapiru*—that is, "Hebrews"—with a stigmatizing tone similar to the way the resistance of the poor is labeled "terrorist" or "communist," with all the satanization those epithets carry in the capitalist ideology of the industrialized countries. Jesus' enemies also considered subversive his proclamation of the kingdom and the signs he worked to make it real.

To express solidarity by restoring the banners of justice and dignity to the resistance of the poor in Central America, their legitimate standard-bearers, is an act of human loyalty that shines with its own goodness. Christian faith interprets this self-evident goodness, flawlessly legitimate on the human level, as meaning adherence to the truth that is built up in the struggle against the enemies of the cause of the poor, those who are "fathers of lies" and "murderers from the beginning," in their connivance with all the ways the self-liberation projects of the poor have been misrepresented throughout history. The truth in question is that which forms the basis for the struggle against all the forces that hold the poor down—a struggle patterned on the preferential fatherhood of the Father of Jesus Christ toward the poor, with the aim that humankind become the fellowship intended in God's plan.

A Self-Evident Goodness

The struggles of the Central American poor have repeatedly unleashed a torrent of fellowship that has not only led to the ultimate witness of love, giving one's life for one's friends, but has also begun to create—in Nicaragua and in parts of El Salvador and Guatemala—new experiences of zest for life and a deep sense of inner peace, and new structures for sharing the goods of this earth. Not all is bloodshed and inhumanity when the poor, striving rightfully to take an active role in shaping history, struggle to create their popular organizations and then to work out their own liberation in history. They have begun to shed the centuries-old mistrust planted in them through the growth of capitalist individualism and the prevailing lies set in place as a barrier to solidarity. In its stead a network of fellowship is taking shape, affirming life in the midst of suffering.

In this glimmering, in this "new dawn"—as they sing in Nicaragua—daily life has begun to take on characteristics of hope that relieve it of its previous overwhelming tendency toward mutual distrust. Here goodness is self-evident and it is expressed in the creative explosion of song to new life, which is even stronger than songs of protest against injustice. In this song to life, reflecting the beginnings of new life in history, there is expressed a conviction that what is being born is legitimate, despite the fact that it is threatened by death, even as it is being born. In its burst of goodness it is like the cry of the infant being born in an Amerindian hut in the Guatemalan highlands, as an expression of hope for life and a life that is better—while right there or next door another child a few months old dies of diphtheria. *Who can doubt that this affirmation of hope in life, with its self-evident and radiant goodness, is good in itself and worthy of a response in solidarity?* And who can doubt that as Christians we have the responsibility of reaffirming it as the commitment of the Father of Jesus to the inextinguishable hope of the poor and as a sacrament of the perfect fellowship that will exist when at the end of history Jesus Christ hands over the kingdom to the Father?

All these situations and processes in history, rooted in the present struggle of the Central America poor and their organized movements—including the tension between vanguard and masses, and sometimes, as in Nicaragua, between vanguard, government, and masses—in their concrete embodiment, whether by what they are trying to put into effect or by their struggle against intolerable limits imposed on human dignity, reflect a goodness that is self-evident. In a sense these factors are "ultimate" and by their very nature demand a response of solidarity. They are "ultimate" in the sense that they point toward elements that are basic to the human condition as it has moved to the center of consciousness in those human groups that have been making history over the centuries. They are ultimate because they are humanizing in history, both insofar as they affirm values of generosity and insofar as they seek to create for those values social and structural conditions that are better than those we now have. They are ultimate especially insofar as they mean that the poor are themselves taking an active role in history with increasing dignity. Indeed, it is precisely the ability to make history that has been denied them by class-structured or bureaucratized national systems and by hegemonic world systems.

To be sure there is tension within this process of the Central American poor in history in its concrete, day-to-day embodiment: some persons strive to move upward (seek the power to dominate), others are afraid of freedom, and still others sometimes act with a heroism that becomes inhuman with its Promethean thrust in history and is unable to accept the weakness of the human condition. The self-evident goodness we have been pointing to is thus marked by ambiguity. This ambiguity is in fact a result of human authenticity that does not idealize the ongoing process of history but is able to take on its powerful hope in both suffering and struggle. Those involved in this process reject naivety vis-à-vis evil, which from within the human condition continually affects even the best efforts to create a new future. Nevertheless it is *from within that ambiguity that the ongoing praxis of the poor constructs a realm of truth* and challenges others to solidarity.

The poor who have died, whether slowly or violently, struggling for their hopes, are themselves a permanent claim on the ongoing course of history. That claim may constitute a reserve of human loyalty that may help preserve what is humanizing and differentiate it from what is dehumanizing in the very process of projecting the future as it is being built. It is not only those who are presently struggling who are active agents challenging their brothers and sisters and demanding a response of solidarity; those who have sacrificed their lives for that hope and those who will inherit the struggle are active agents as well.

To this challenge, which is a cry for shared life, liberty, and justice, Christian faith is committed because of the foreshadowings of Jesus Christ implanted in the history of our world from its beginning. To discover these foreshadowings, these groanings of the Spirit (Rom. 8:18—27), within the movements of the poor in history—and today in the struggles of Central America—and stand in solidarity with them is a Christian duty. But it is a Christian duty shot through with hope, for we believe that the Lord Jesus draws all history to himself, not only from its beginning but also from the absolute future, in which the firstborn is the risen Jesus. And we believe that he "will give a new form to this lowly body of ours and remake it according to the pattern of his glorified body, by his power to subject everything to himself" (Phil. 3:21).

In tension with that Christian faith and hope with which many of us are called to carry out the work of love called solidarity, we must first locate that task in the material reality of the self-liberation projects of the Central American poor, which today challenge us and demand such solidarity on the basis of the self-evident goodness present in their march forward in history. By paying attention to the material reality challenging us to solidarity we may perhaps be able to take on solidarity with the *humility* appropriate for those who have not been the only ones—nor the first—to shed blood for the life of the poor, whom we always have "with us." Our solidarity will thus find itself challenged to "do right and love goodness," so as to "walk humbly with [our] . . . God" in history (Mic. 6:8).

Responding to this challenge will also make it easier for those of us who make up the church to seek the Lord not of the church only but of the church and of history, Jesus of Nazareth arisen, a lordship that both stands over and is exercised within the self-liberation undertakings of the poor in history. This brings us to our next line of thought where we shall view solidarity from the viewpoint of the church as it faces those processes.

Christian Solidarity: The Distinguishing Note
of Unity and Loyalty between Churches

Because of the biblical roots of its faith and its very identity and because it is set in the midst of humankind and has a call to accept the poor of this world in an absolute manner, the church should be noted for its attitude toward and praxis of solidarity with the cause of the poor and with its translation into concrete deeds in history, despite all their ambiguity and precariousness. In the next section of this study we shall look at how this distinctive kind of solidarity demands conversion on the part of the church. In the present section we shall be considering *the proper place for solidarity between local churches* so as to forge true unity and love that is loyal to the end, both of which are traits that make up the heart of the new community that Jesus wanted to create, starting with his immediate followers.

Radical Universality

In the New Testament these followers are viewed as "the twelve apostles" (or simply "the twelve") so as to show that Jesus' new community is the recipient of the promises God made to Israel, Jesus himself being the "definitive yes" (2 Cor. 1:19). For its part John's Gospel presents the new community of Jesus in a different way in passages such as his last chapter, where the risen Jesus appears to seven disciples (John 21). As is well known, John's Gospel often makes use of the symbolism of numbers, but the point is never simply numbers in a quantitative sense. As a symbol of totality, the number seven, applied to Jesus' followers, in contrast to "the twelve," denotes the new community of Jesus. It thus signals that it has not only received the promises as its inheritance but that it is also open to the universality of all peoples and open to all the germinal christic orientations present in them, the seed of Jesus Christ sown in them from the creation, and open to the perfect justice of the kingdom. Jesus crucified and risen, the first consummate fruit of this justice of the kingdom, draws all persons toward a greater and better future in history (without this being equivalent to an ideology of linear progress).

This openness of the new community that Jesus convoked and called into existence, which leads it to enclose in its embrace the people of Israel and all peoples, is what constitutes the *radical universality* of the church of Jesus Christ. Paul reflects this universality with his stubborn defense of his mission to the gentiles (non-Israelites) and with the symbol he applies to the Christian community, the symbol of "new humanity" ("new creation") and "new human being" ("new creature") (Col. 3:10; Eph. 2:15; Gal. 6:15; 2 Cor. 5:17). In this symbol all the universality present in humankind insofar as it is the fruit of God's creation—hence excluding nothing—is transferred to the Christian community, the new humanity, wherein the first creation is consummated through the life, death, and resurrection of Jesus, communicated in the Spirit. The conclusion of the Gospel of Matthew (28:19) and many passages of the Gospel of John (1:12; 3:16—17; 10:16; 12:20—21, etc.) bear witness to the same radical universality of the new community created by Jesus.

Social Diversity

One consequence of this radical universality is social diversity—the incorporation into this new community of both citizens and slaves of the Roman empire. The church welcomed the greatest extremes of wealth and poverty during the historical period when the first Christian communities were being formed. Similarly in our own period in history the consequence of this universality is that faith in Jesus Christ is confessed by ecclesial communities in industrialized countries that enjoy affluence and share political hegemony and the shaping of ideas, and also by ecclesial communities rooted in countries whose industry is scant and poor, where there is want and even misery, countries that have little power in international political relationships or over the flow of ideas. Nevertheless, each of these ecclesial communities (national, regional, local) is called to embody the fullness of the "community of Jesus Christ" that being church means.

Just as Paul addressed one of his letters to "the church of God which is in Corinth" (1 Cor. 1:2), today we can speak of the church that is in Guatemala or France, in El Salvador or Holland, in Nicaragua or Australia. We can go on to speak of churches in all human aggregations that in some meaningful way share common characteristics: the church that is in Latin America or Europe, the church that is in Aguilares (a small Salvadoran town where the Jesuit Rutilio Grande ministered and where he was murdered in 1977), and in the state of Israel (where scarcely two hundred Jewish Catholics confess faith in Jesus Christ), and finally, the church that is in this or that grassroots community.

Preponderance of the Lowly

Radical universality must be qualified by the unquestionable fact that Jesus called the first community of his disciples from among men and women who for the most part came from the strata of those who were poor or ostracized by the society of his time—just as faith in Yahweh crystalized around a people that originated from groupings that were impoverished and dominated. Such was the pattern of the social makeup of Christian communities, at least until their religion began to be tolerated by society at large, and then, from Constantine onward, became the religion of the empire.

Paul's statements about the Christian community at Corinth would not have to be twisted in order to be applied to most members of other Christian communities during the early centuries:

> Not many of you are wise, as men account wisdom; not many are influential; and surely not many are well-born. God chose those whom the world considers absurd to shame the wise; he singled out the weak of this world to shame the strong. He chose the world's lowborn and despised, those who count for nothing, to reduce to nothing those who were something: so that mankind can do no boasting before God [1 Cor. 1:26–29].

What is important about these statements is that Paul wrote them to a community perhaps made up mainly of dock-workers in the port of Corinth, most of whom were of pagan origin. They had internalized the hierarchy of values of the dominant group in that prosperous Greek city, the commercial hub of the Mediterranean. These lines were written from a Christian sense of equality among human beings, an awareness that elsewhere prompts Paul to say that in Jesus Christ all differences of rank have been broken: between Jews and pagans, between the enslaved and the free, between Roman citizens and foreigners, between man and woman (1 Cor. 12:13; Gal. 3:18; Col. 3:11). These lines also reflect the awareness that makes Paul angry over the inability of the community to surmount social inequality even in the eucharistic celebration of the Lord's supper (1 Cor. 11:20–22, 27)

Above, in the second section of this study, we saw how in John's Gospel this equality becomes programatic in the foot washing (John 13:1–20) and how it is viewed from the perspective of the poor (John 12:1–18). The same equality is joyfully witnessed in the Acts of the Apostles where it takes the form of "holding all things in common" as a verification of the truth of shared prayer and eucharist (Acts 2:42–47; 4:32–35). By the same token inequality is severely denounced in Acts (5:1–11) and in the letter of James (1:9–11; 2:1–9).

Equality and Co-Responsibility

Many of the assertions of equality made from the perspective of the poor are aimed fundamentally either at the whole new community created by Jesus or at local communities. *The universality of this call to human beings who differ from one another owning to their origins (religious, racial, cultural, social, sexual, etc.) is Christian and really ecclesial only when believers advance toward a new alternative of personal and social life where equality prevails and life is being built up through solidarity.* That is why holding possessions in common and standing in co-responsibility for the sufferings and joys of brothers and sisters is the basic attitude that Paul repeatedly urges: "Help carry one another's burdens," "bearing with one another," "bear with one another" (Gal. 6:2; Eph. 4:2; Col. 3:13). This attitude extends from sharing the knowledge of God to sharing material goods.

For Paul the grounding of this attitude is unquestionably found in the following of Jesus of Nazareth, the Messiah, as he puts it in one of the most forceful passages of exhortation in all his letters: "let all parties think humbly of others as superior to themselves, each of you looking to others' interests rather than to his own. Your attitude must be that of Christ" (Phil. 2:3b–5). This attitude is exactly the same as what we saw in the foot washing: Jesus "put off his rank and became one among many" to the point of giving his life, executed for the cause of equality and love between human beings, because he had lived his life from the perspective of a love that took sides with the poor and the ostracized in a society that could not tolerate such a stance either religiously or politically.

Universality Tested by Solidarity

If, continuing to follow Paul, we pass from considering this program as intended for the whole of the new and universal community of Jesus and from focusing on the relationships within particular Christian communities, to the question of relationships between different church communities, we see that the *universality* he has defended in order to call pagans to conversion and to establish Christian communities *will be tested in the fire of solidarity*. In the letter to the Galatians Paul describes how he boldly challenged the other apostles in Jerusalem in order to defend Christian freedom regarding the religious and cultural customs of the people of Israel, and especially in order to defend the idea that God's gift is universal and is not restricted to the Jews (Gal. 2:1–21). There Paul states that "James and Peter and John," when they accepted the mission of Paul and Barnabas to the pagans, requested only "that we should be mindful of the poor in Jerusalem— the one thing that I was making every effort to do" (Gal. 2:9–

10). Plainly no mission could be Christian if it was not validated through fulfillment of the commandment of love lived in solidarity with the Christian communities in Jerusalem, which were quite poor, and those of Asia and Greece, perhaps less in need.

In fact, Paul goes on to write several letters reminding the various Christian communities in Greece of the *campaign of solidarity with the poor churches of Jerusalem* that he himself had started when he visited them. In the second letter to the Corinthians some fragments of these exhortations of Paul are preserved and they constitute a *whole theology of solidarity between the churches*. First, Paul tries to stimulate a Christian rivalry between the different churches around the distinctive Christian trait of solidarity. He tells the Corinthians: "Brothers, I should like you to know of the grace of God conferred on the churches of Macedonia. In the midst of severe trial their overflowing joy and deep poverty have produced an abundant generosity" (2 Cor. 8:1–2).

As we shall see later, it would seem that the situation of Christians in Corinth is not one of misery, or at any rate some of them stand in less need (1 Cor. 11:20–22). Paul wants to make Christians who are less poor aware of their duty to show solidarity to the people of God in Jerusalem who are living in penury. In order to stimulate them he tells them how very poor communities, even though undergoing great trials themselves, have responded to this appeal for solidarity with abundant generosity, and have done so, he says, with overflowing joy. Paul indeed says that God's gift to the communities in Macedonia has consisted precisely in the fact that, although their poverty is extreme and could lead to self-pity and resentment, they have lived it not with passive resignation but with an active and overflowing joy that unleashed a torrent of fellowship so as to provide relief for the needs of others. Those needs were perhaps no greater than their own but were more devastating in their effect. And they did this in solidarity—that is, without loss of dignity to anyone.

Thus, through solidarity between the churches, the life-affirming alternative created by Jesus in the new community of his followers does what it is meant to do by acting as a

ferment in the midst of any liberation undertaking in history.
Within the liberative self-projection of the colonized society
of Judea under the Roman empire, the solidarity of the
churches means both relieving want and denouncing a merci-
less system, both of which are forms of struggle for justice
and equality. It is as a mirroring of such attitudes that the
Christian writer Tertullian, living in the heart of the Roman
empire, cites the witness of persons of good will when they
observe Christians and say, "See how they love one another!"
Even making allowance for the apologetic and polemical
thrust of this remark, comparing the lifestyle of Roman society with that of the Christian community, it is highly unlikely that he would have made such a statement in a writing
that could certainly fall into the hands of imperial censors
unless it had a basis in fact.

Hence at least in the third century we find evidence that in
Christian communities persons are to some extent living up
to Jesus' charge: "This is how all will know you for my disciples: your love for one another." That testimony may be used
for judging the effectiveness of the bold statement that John
has Jesus make about all who will relate to him in the future
(bold because it expresses a real possibility of living a life
spent in love), with unconcern for self and concern for others:
"I have given them the glory you gave me that they may be
one, as we are one" (John 17:22). Jesus's "glory," which
makes him equal to the Father, is that of being "filled with
enduring love" (John 1:14), or (Septuagint) "full of love and
truth," or "fidelity." The words of the Greek text, *charis* and
aletheia, translate the Hebrew words *hesed* and *emert*, which
the Old Testament regularly applies to the indestructibly
faithful love of Yahweh for Israel and for the poor of Israel.

Because in Jesus of Nazareth this "enduring love" goes to
the extreme of a life given up for humankind (a life spent announcing the good news of the kingdom to the poor and defending their cause), Christian solidarity between the
churches should have as its possible and real horizon "laying
down one's life for one's friends" as the pinnacle of love (John
15:12–13). It could also result from the hatred of a system
that is opposed to fellowship and to equality between human

beings because it is geared to the god of wealth (John 15:20–25; 7:1–7; 2:13–22; 5:16, etc.)

To live sharing everything, from the knowledge of God, to a practical sympathy with the sufferings of others, to holding material goods in common, is a life-affirming alternative. It can act as a ferment for any liberative projection in history, not out of hatred and resentment but out of the joy that comes from the struggle for fellowship and justice. Such a life-affirming alternative is intolerable for any system of injustice and domination (that is, for "the world," in the texts from John's Gospel just cited). Practicing it with utter seriousness may end in martyrdom.

About ten priests who came from other national churches to work in the church in Guatemala have been murdered for the cause of solidarity with the people of God, especially with those who were poor and were struggling for fellowship and justice. In El Salvador and all throughout Latin America other priests, and lay persons and religious sisters as well, have carried their solidarity all the way to the extreme of an unbreakably faithful and loyal love for the hope of the poor. Most of them came from churches in countries that live in affluence, but many had known poverty in the midst of the affluence.

In his letter to the Corinthians, which we are using for this reflection on solidarity between churches, Paul appeals to this same glory of God, made visible and tangible in the life of Jesus Christ, the Lord. After stimulating the Corinthians by speaking of the generosity of the Christian communities of Macedonia, Paul speaks to them of the abundant spiritual goods they enjoy: "just as you are rich in every respect, in faith and discourse, in knowledge, in total concern, and in the love we bear you" (2 Cor. 8:7).

Paul draws the conclusion in a manner similar to Jesus' reply to the "rich young man" mentioned in the Gospels (Matt. 16:29 and parallels)—that is, Paul tells the Corinthians that if sharing in spiritual goods and their abundance is to be verified as true and believable in a Christian way, it must be translated into a sharing of material goods: "so may you abound in this charity" (2 Cor. 8:7). As the letter continues, the aim of this abounding solidarity, which is to relieve the want of brothers and sisters, reappears: being consistent with true Christian practice and with the life of Christ, who is followed in such practice:

> I am not giving an order but simply testing your generous love against the concern which others show. You are well acquainted with the favor shown you by our Lord Jesus Christ; how for your sake he made himself poor though he was rich so that you might become rich by his poverty [2 Cor. 8:8–9].

Thus solidarity, which means sharing everything—from faith in Jesus Christ to material goods—is not a set of rules that can be set out as norms or a discipline regulating relationships between churches. It is rather a demand that is inherent in the following of Jesus Christ, Lord of the church; it is a gift that enriches the one to whom it is given but also the one who practices it. In terms of church unity, *solidarity is the distinctive note validating the truth of the universality of the church with the authenticity of the following of Jesus Christ.*

As we have already noted about the community in Corinth, although its members had little education, power, or prestige, it must not have been in such dire material circumstances as was the church in Jerusalem. Hence, although he has prodded the community in Corinth with the amazingly generous solidarity of the communities in Macedonia, which are indeed afflicted with great want, Paul ultimately bases his appeal for solidarity with the church in Jerusalem on the *equality* that should be present in the life-affirming alternative that the new community of Jesus represents in opposition to systems of injustice and domination:

> The relief of others ought not to impoverish you; there should be a certain equality. Your plenty at the present time should supply their need so that their surplus may one day supply your need, with equality as the result. It is written, "he who gathered much had no excess and he who gathered little had no lack" [2 Cor. 8:13–15].

It is quite likely that the text from Exodus (16:18) here quoted by Paul, as also his interpretation of it in letter, goes back to the faith of Israel as deepened by the historical experience of the group of liberated slaves who migrated to Canaan and struggled against the danger of individualistic accumulation of wealth during their long march. That danger obviously threatened the ideal of freedom in justice and equality that they had inherited from the struggle against the injustice and exploitation of slavery. Justice and equality had been demanded both by Yahweh and by the very nature of their historical struggles.

Moreover, the Exodus passage cited by Paul—that is, the narrative accounts of how the former slaves were fed with "manna" as they migrated toward Canaan—have been seen in the New Testament tradition as a symbol of the eucharistic meal (John 6:29–37, 47–58), as the meal that builds unity as it builds Christian community in the following of Jesus Christ the Lord, which means taking on the same life and the same kind of practice as his. Thus it is not surprising that Paul is scandalized by the social inequalities manifesting anti-solidarity that are obvious even in the eucharist in the Corinthian community (1 Cor. 11:20–22). Therefore, "whoever eats the bread or drinks the cup of the Lord unworthily"—that is, without practicing in their life the solidarity celebrated and made real in the eucharist—"sins against the body and blood of the Lord" (1 Cor. 11:27).

In another section of the letter we are discussing (in fact, a section that, according to experts, originally was another shorter letter in its own right) Paul once again insists that a collection be taken up to show solidarity with the church in Jerusalem. This letter is earlier than the one we have been quoting from, as can be seen from the fact that Paul says he has created a rivalry between the communities of Macedonia with the example of solidarity already given by Christians of the Corinthian community. This rivalry was so effective that Paul was later able to go on to prod the generosity of the Corinthian community with the example of the extraordinary generosity of the communities of Macedonia, as we have seen. Paul has no doubt that the result of the abnegation and austerity implied in that solidarity will lead to an enrichment of those who offer it—an enrichment that will be all the greater the more generous is this leaven of solidarity (2 Cor. 9:6–11). A further result of solidarity, Paul goes on to say, will be God's glory—that is, validation of the credibility of the faith held by Christians: there will be "much gratitude to God" if their practice is coherent with the good news of Jesus Christ, which they have obeyed and made concrete in generous solidarity.

Finally the recompense of those who have practiced solidarity is that they will be remembered in prayer by those to whom they have become more deeply related as brothers and sisters (2 Cor. 9:12–15). Paul unambiguously links the faithful hearing of the good news—the gospel of Jesus Christ—to practical solidarity, expressed in a generous and enduring love toward the poor, and so doing justice to the messianic portent: "he has sent me to bring glad tidings to the poor" (Luke 4:18; cf. Isa. 61:1)—a praxis the churches are obligated to continue. If they do not do so, they do not validate God's enduring love, which is invincibly loyal to the hope of the poor. If they do so, their solidarity will be in the midst of "the world"—that is, in the midst of a whole system of injustice and domination that does all it can to perpetuate poverty. Such solidarity will be the best "apologetics"—that is, the best validation of the credibility of their faith in God within human history.

Secularization and Dehumanization

The question of how churches are to relate to one another is today bound up with two other major concerns that stand in unresolved conflict. On the one hand there is concern over *secularization* in both the Western capitalist world and in the Eastern socialist world. This concern takes cognizance of the humanistic element in secularization and seeks to establish between the churches a solidarity in terms of "bearing with one another" the responsibility for vindicating God in history, something necessary in the long run for a sober exaltation of the human being. The other concern has to do with the *dehumanization of humankind and especially of the poor,* due to the growing unjust impoverishment of vast masses of the human race and of entire peoples, the abuse of power and authority that refuses to regard all peoples as equal in the family of nations, and the bloody repression that seeks to frustrate the quest for justice and equality that destitute and debilitated peoples attempt to carry out in history. This dehumanization of the poor, often practiced by systems that appeal to Christian tradition for their justification, is recognized as an attack on the God of Jesus Christ. Concern for dehumanization seeks to establish between the churches a solidarity "bearing with one another" the responsibility of validating the poor and their liberative undertakings in history, without which there is no validation of God in history.

In the sharp opposition between these two ecclesial emphases having to do with solidarity there is a danger of falling into the trap of a "worldly" way of addressing the problem, one created by the systems that dispute the hegemony of the planet. The two schools of thought square off for intellectual debate. Christian solidarity is then *ideologized*, and thus neutralized, in an internal contradiction provoked by interests contrary to the cause of Jesus, the cause of the kingdom. For it is plain in the whole biblical tradition we have been recalling here that solidarity between churches extends to sharing every kind of good—communion in both spiritual and material goods. In maintaining one or the other opinion as to how solidarity is best exercised, it is obvious that there will be oppositions between values sought to be upheld and guarded as priorities when they are seen to be threatened with resistance. Concern over secularization is particularly sensitive to *justice* that humanizes. But it is equally clear that when these emphases are put in opposition to each other, solidarity between churches is trapped in the ideology of struggle for hegemony. For freedom without justice is freedom for the rich and powerful, and its fruits are an overt or covert crushing of the poor. And justice without freedom is a betrayal of the dignity of the poor, no matter what idealism or rhetoric is used to cover it up.

Nevertheless, *the solution to the problem of solidarity be-*

tween churches is not to be found in an easy reconciling of opposites—even when these "opposites" have been twisted ideologically so as to make them such. The answer is rather to be found in the Christian way that Jesus, inheriting and going beyond both the Yahwistic legacy of Israel and the experience of his people in history, affirms the universality that is proper to God, his Father. This is a universality that takes on a preferential identification with the poor and the weak who are crucified in history and so, through a paradoxical detour that passes by way of partiality toward the poor and their cause, fosters a universality that gradually increases fellowship in the world.

Solidarity between churches should be understood and practiced primarily from this perspective, the perspective of the crucified Son of God, of the many faces of Christ, crucified today but also committed to the struggle for life that comes from the impulse of the Spirit, who keeps alive the memory of Jesus crucified and risen. From this perspective, in the concern aroused by the fact that Jesus is being crucified in the present reality of the crucifixion of whole populations of the poor in their immense masses—*made up of persons and not subhuman beings*—at the same time that the hope of the poor is being salvaged, church solidarity must validate the ultimate foundation and guarantee of that hope: God's love, unalterably steadfast and faithful to human beings and their history.

From the perspective of the demand for justice and for equal political participation by the poor, there must also be a demand for the dignity that cannot exist without freedom. *That is why solidarity between churches, if it is Christian solidarity, crucifies.* That is why the powers of this world label and stigmatize it as "naivety" and as going along with "communism," that contemporary variety of satanism that one is expected to acknowledge and fear more than God, and so to attack it with any available means, however inhuman they may be.

The concrete history of solidarity between the Christian churches of England, France, Spain, Germany, the United States, and Canada with the churches of the poor in Nicaragua, El Salvador, and Guatemala is a history that with increasing intensity is creating the interchurch solidarity I have attempted to reclaim, starting from passages of Paul in the second letter to the Corinthians. In this ongoing history there is a "bearing with one another" on the part of the churches in a renewed effort of fidelity to the cause of the justice of the kingdom in the midst of present history. Archbishop Romero and the other martyrs of the churches in Central America, and the very authenticity of those oppressed Central American believing peoples (an authenticity that is always precarious and sinful), aroused this solidarity and so made it possible for many churches in rich countries to receive God's gift of risking impoverishment in order to enrich the poor and be enriched by them. The gain has been reflected in the meaning of faith for today, intensified prayer for one another, and goods shared and held in common. But there is still a long way to go in the practice of interchurch solidarity.

Solidarity, Key to the Conversion of the Church and the Recovery of Its Role as Prophet and Servant

At the end of the previous section we devoted some thought to what may be one of the greatest temptations affecting the solidarity of the churches and solidarity between churches, a temptation that risks twisting and ideologizing solidarity to serve "worldly" interests. This is not the only temptation the churches face as they practice solidarity. Others include making solidarity sectarian, utilizing and manipulating solidarity in order to increase some power the church has that is not specifically Christian, relinquishing the evangelizing and prophetic sense of solidarity, and, finally, controlling and misusing solidarity, rather than practicing the gospel vigilance that church authorities ought to maintain. On the basis of what we have already said we are now going to look into these aspects, these tests by fire, in which the solidarity of the church can be purified. They have provided many real opportunities for the church to be converted and to recover its own identity in a purified form.

Conversion of the Church

We have seen above how the God in whom we believe, the
God of Jesus Christ, arouses faith through the crisis experienced by individuals and whole peoples when they must
face the choice between alternate undertakings in history,
which in the Bible are seen both as a divine gift and a human
task. We have also reflected on how these projected undertakings in history are either basically good or evil and that in
general (not ignoring other factors entailing ambiguity) evidence of their moral character is clear for those who have
opted for humankind from the perspective of those whose
suffering, weakness, and impoverishment are recognized as
intolerable and unjust. We know that this kind of evidence
brings us to a fork in the road: from our Christian faith we
interpret this as both the seed of Jesus Christ sown by God in
all humankind when it was first created, and also as the attraction that Jesus Christ, through the Spirit, exercises on
history from his life, death, and resurrection. In addition, we
are quite aware that most Central Americans are both oppressed and believers in Jesus Christ, with a faith that is,
willy-nilly, related to the church.

From this perspective, to make church solidarity sectarian
would mean to give in to the temptation to consider the
churches in Central America to be the sole or the main object
of solidarity. But if we are to be faithful to God's design of
remaining utterly faithful to the hope of the poor, the main
(though not exclusive) object of the solidarity of the churches
in Central America must be the liberative self-projections of
the poor in history—that is, the liberative undertakings that
are viable in history and offer the greatest guarantees that
they may serve as a channel for the hope of the poor.

Showing interchurch solidarity in favor of the church in
Central America and with the lot of its bishops, priests, men
and women religious, and its organizations is legitimate only
insofar as the churches there are clearly verifying their faith
in a practical manner that makes them a "sacrament or sign
of intimate union with God, and of the unity of all humankind" (*Lumen Gentium,* 1). In their underlying identity as

church they will be a "sign of intimate union with God" if their proclamation of the word, their community-building, and their worship make credible God's enduring love for the poor, because they are centered on striving for what is just and right, and for that equality in fellowship that is Jesus' last command and legacy. They will be a "sign and instrument of the unity of all humankind" inserted into the midst of unfolding history if they are a sign and instrument of, or at least a humble contribution to, the unity of the Central American poor in a historical thrust forward in a way that consolidates their hope. For not every kind of unity is free from the tendency of some human beings to subjugate others and violate their dignity, whether subtly or brutally.

For example, when Oscar Romero was archbishop of San Salvador, the church of God there, despite its human precariousness and ambiguity, carried out Jesus Christ's command to follow him and was faithful to his God. What Paul said to the Christian community of Galatia is also relevant for solidarity with the liberative programs of the poor in Central America in the case of the church of San Salvador and also for other communities trying to serve the justice of the kingdom, although perhaps with greater weakness and ambiguity: "While we have the opportunity, let us do good to all men—but especially those of the household of the faith" (Gal. 6:10). Paul's use of "especially" here retains all its meaning, whether the sister churches are actually proving their faithfulness, or whether they need the surging of solidarity to be converted.

Giving priority to the liberative undertakings of the Central American poor in history (as the main object of solidarity) entails a conversion on the part of the church, a conversion that consists in *ceasing to be centered on itself*, and when it seeks solidarity from other churches, *centering its appeal on helping the whole people to move toward the kingdom*. It is from this perspective of the poor as a people moving toward closer approximations of the kingdom that the churches, setting aside any sense of being a group set apart or a sect of the pure, will have to *accompany* the poor and their organizations as a whole people. The very mention of this *pastoral role of accompaniment* (proper to the whole community of the church, although with differentiated functions) is a direct reminder of one of the tasks of the church that Archbishop Romero rediscovered and emphasized.

This solidarity should not be inordinately focused on the church, either in requests from churches in Central America to churches in other regions, or in their response of solidarity. The churches should remain centered on the liberative undertakings of the poor in history, once they have discerned in the Spirit that these undertakings serve the hope of the poor. That ambiguities may be found there is a reason for maintaining prophetic vigilance but should not be a pretext for deflecting the church from the central aim of solidarity.

Obviously none of what we have been saying negates in any way that other (and quite legitimate) kind of solidarity that some churches show toward others in order to help each other with their own special obligation—proclaiming Jesus Christ, building community, and celebrating life. For Christian communities today in Central America that kind of solidarity is made more urgent by the very fact that they are more subject to persecution, precisely because more and more of those communities are gradually taking on the cause of the poor.

Life-giving Service

In this study we have been paying particular attention to the fact that Jesus sought to make the new community he was creating a life-giving alternative, set in the midst of the power systems that appear one after another in history. A life-giving alternative, not a power alternative—that is what the new community of Jesus Christ, the church, is called to be in history. That is why in the foot washing we can see how Jesus was building this community in such a way that, *by means of service,* it would be a leaven of equality, freedom, justice—in a word, of dignity—in the midst of human society in history. In doing so Jesus takes on himself the historical propulsion of Israel toward justice, but he changes the exclusive way this drive is embodied and turns it into a leavening force in the midst of the nations. That obviously does not mean that living out a political vocation in concrete courses of action in history and being committed to their causes may not be a valid way for Christians to follow Jesus Christ.

On the basis of what we have established thus far, we may say that using and manipulating solidarity in order to acquire or increase some power that is not specifically Christian means making a *subtle and hypocritical use of solidarity* in order to retain—as one power vis-à-vis another—a hold over the way the liberative program of the poor in Central America takes shape, a hold that is real in cultural and political terms. Deep down the aim is to put a new face on what has been known historically as "Christendom." To do so there is negotiation—implicitly—for power agreements, for sharing power, on the basis of an already accumulated capital: the ability to draw solidarity toward the self-liberative projects of the poor in history. Moreover, there is an effort to keep hold of this influence and this bargaining power by obtaining aid or development funds from church solidarity sources, enabling the church to retain a financial hold over the people and over the apparatus of power in society. When church officials act in this way, projects originally intended to contribute to the forward thrust of the poor in history and to provide a real service to the poor by the church, end up being changed into "parallel" undertakings or even beachheads ready to be utilized against the liberative projects of the poor in history.

Again Archbishop Romero's pastoral insights (the crystalization of the cry and the hope of the poor, his people) are very illuminating and should help the churches avoid this covert temptation to power. When he spoke on "the political dimension of faith" in Louvain a month and a half before being martyred, he was clear:

> The point is not that the church considers itself a political institution in competition with other political groups, or that it has its own political mechanisms; even less is it the case that our church wants to exercise political leadership. What is at stake is something deeper and more evangelical: making a true option for the poor,

being incarnate in their world, announcing the good news to them, giving them hope, stimulating them to a liberating praxis, defending their cause and sharing their fate. . . . Because it has opted for the real poor and not a fictitious version . . . and for those who are really oppressed and repressed, the church lives in the political sphere and is realized as church through the political sphere [*La voz de los sin voz: La palabra viva de Monseñor Romero,* San Salvador, UCA Ed., 1980, 188–90].

That there is no intention of holding onto some vestige of church paternalism in providing aid for the poor is made unmistakably clear later in his speech:

The world of the poor teaches us that liberation will arrive when the poor are not simply the objects of benefits conferred by governments or even by the church, but are themselves agents and protagonists of their struggle and their liberation, thus unmasking false paternalisms, even those practiced by the church [ibid., 192].

Finally, with this same clearsightedness, Archbishop Romero points to the consequences for the identity of the church:

I have sought to clarify for you the ultimate criterion, which is based on theology and ongoing history, for the activity of the church in this field [the socio-political]: the world of the poor. According to the way they, the poor as a people, are affected, *the church will continue to give its support to one political project or another, while remaining within its specific role* [ibid., 193; italics added].

The criterion of this support for such undertakings is therefore not the good of the church, and certainly not its acquiring or increasing power, but rather the good of the poor. This is true both for the church in areas where liberative projects are being attempted and for churches elsewhere that stand in solidarity. The criterion for solidarity with such projects, both in their adequacy in relation to current history and from a theological viewpoint, is not how they might affect the church, but how they affect the poor. In this fashion the church will really continue in an attitude of service through solidarity. In this fashion, like Jesus, the incarnate Son of God, it will share the same lot as the poor. In this fashion it will keep alive faith in the God and Father of Jesus Christ, who is invincibly faithful to the hope-filled dignity of the poor, and whose "glory is the life of the poor." This is ultimately how the church will keep its identity a leaven within historical processes, as an alternate way of life, challenging every form of domination and oppressive power.

Solidarity: Mission

The solidarity of churches with the forward march of the poor in Central America, precisely because it is not solidarity with the cause of the poor in abstraction, nor (even less) only with human rights violated in individual poor persons, must be a solidarity that humbly retains its prophetic capacity, and it should never shrink from exercising that solidarity in the name of Jesus Christ. This is so, not only because it is the mission of the church to evangelize—and if I may paraphrase Paul, "Woe to the church, if it does not announce the good news of Jesus Christ" (1 Cor. 9:16)—but also because most Central Americans are at once impoverished, dominated, and believers in Jesus Christ. The solidarity of the church with their undertakings in history must be carried out in the name of Jesus Christ, so that the purpose of seeking to end hunger may not be perverted into depriving persons of the bread of their faith and of the ultimate guarantee of their hope.

We have already considered the fact that the liberative programs of the poor in history, despite their self-evident goodness, are also shrouded in an ambiguity that might lead them off track. We must reject every type of naivety vis-à-vis the evil that continually assaults any attempt to construct a better future, and make its way in, corrupting to a greater or

lesser extent. The human condition is such that evil sometimes stands in insuperable contradiction to human goodness (what Paul means when he says that "creation was made
subject to futility, not of its own accord, but by him who once
subjected it"—Rom. 8:19–20).

To abdicate the evangelical and prophetical thrust of ecclesial solidarity means to renounce the most specific element
of the mission of the church: pronouncing the name of Jesus
within history. It means to refuse to retell the story of Jesus
every time the church is asked to contribute to the birth of
something new in history, or to radically renew what is old. It
is a Christian conviction, one that can be quite scandalous,
that faith in Jesus of Nazareth crucified and arisen has the
power to humanize history. This conviction is grounded in
belief that ongoing history can in fact be good because from
creation onward Jesus Christ is sown in it like a seed and
stands like a magnetic pole, drawing all things toward an ever
greater future, inasmuch as he has been made lord of history
by his life, death, and resurrection. To withhold from the liberative undertakings of the poor this life that is the remem-
brance of all Jesus said and did, even while humbly providing
the bread of solidarity, is to withhold from them what can be a
living source of humanization. But it also amounts to depriving faith in Jesus Christ, and in the God and Father of Jesus
Christ, of the chance to become greater and better, ever
younger, by being professed in a new manner from within yet
another attempt by the poor to better approximate the justice
of the kingdom. *For us Central Americans church solidarity is
also "mission"—the church sent out within history.*

Only the most incredibly naive could fail to see that a liberation process that sees itself constrained to engage in a war—
even if it be a just war—can lead to dehumanizing results.
Only through naive enthusiasm (which will later take its toll in
bitter disappointment) can one fail to recognize the risk there
is in pursuing any such process such as in building up hope
that the Sandinista project in Nicaragua as a self-projection
of the poor in history can be paradigmatic for other parts of
Latin America and for oppressed populations elsewhere. This
risk is built into the need to balance freedom and justice,

firmness and compassion, defense and work, and pardoning, using power responsibly and boldly, or using it too freely or too timidly, and so forth.

The Christian churches owe solidarity to the struggle of the poor in El Salvador and Guatemala, and to the defense of what the poor in Nicaragua are doing. In fact, if the Spirit, in true discernment, so inclines them, they might even point to the leadership of these historical processes, their vanguards, as present-day "Cyruses," as leaders who are anointed with a mission that has something to do with advancing toward the kingdom, whether those leadership groups are aware of it or not—that is, whether or not they are consciously fulfilling a political vocation that is inspired by Christian faith. (In Isaiah 41:1–4, 44:28, and 45:1–3 Cyrus, the Persian king, is referred to as one who is "anointed" by the Lord to carry out a mission in history.)

However, the churches must never lose sight of the fact that the purpose of any mission in history is to provide an avenue for the hope of the poor. It is not the organizations or the revolutionary vanguards but the poor as a people, themselves increasingly the makers of their own history, who must be the object of the solidarity efforts of the churches. It is a fact that such a people can be seduced into abdicating its self-directive role and passing it on to a leadership group that has gained a reputation for heroism. In solidarity with such leadership and in disinterested service, the churches will find better conditions for exercising the prophetic role of the kingdom and recalling the memory of Jesus. His good news cannot be withheld from the whole people of the poor without curtailing the deepest aspect of ecclesial mission. On occasion, this prophetical role will have to be embodied in a call to the kind of discipline that every organized project in history demands, a discipline sometimes rejected in the name of a freedom that veers toward anarchy. Freedom without authority is the fruit of the kingdom when it is consummated, not of the journey toward the kingdom.

Archbishop Romero had a deep awareness of this mission of the church and maintained an independence that was so authentically Christian that he was able to communicate it to many members of his ecclesial community in San Salvador. For being at the service of the liberative self-projection of the poor in history can never mean falling into the temptation of allowing the mission of the church to be absorbed into the mission of the organizations of the poor. Humility in service rendered by the church and in Christians is precisely what safeguards that independence. When it appears, such independence is self-evident and can easily be distinguished from yearnings for power and hidden influence in the building up of society, yearnings that indeed are not Christian.

Solidarity and Uncertainty

That the self-liberative undertakings of the poor in history are not the product of vague designs for society or of hopes that are mere nostalgia or wishful thinking is something we have seen above. Similarly we have considered how every period of time offers an opportunity for grace (a *kairos*) or for evil in history. Faced with such alternatives, human decisions—and among them, the decision of faith working through love—become problematic.

Sometimes those responsible for hierarchical functions in the church attempt to control the solidarity of churches both in relation to the liberative programs of the poor in history and in their evaluation of the contemporary period. To do so, they convert such programs into abstract constructs, and for the concrete aspiration of flesh-and-blood persons they substitute vague expectations, which conceivably could be realized in many different frameworks, or they give the impression that the degrees of corruption and evil in existing alternatives are really so similar that none of them can be proposed as a specific option to be made through a Christian decision. When church officials use this method of control they are not simply refusing to identify such projects and achievements in history with the consummation of the kingdom—for the church must always refuse to do that, or the faith would be trivialized or falsified. Rather the method of control consists in making reference to the unimaginable goodness that will come into history (but utterly surpassing history) when the Son "will hand over the kingdom to God the Father" (1 Cor. 15:14). This then becomes a motive for skepticism toward, or disdain for, any particular undertaking in history. There is an even subtler kind of control that consists in claiming that the gospel is a source of concrete knowledge of how society should be organized; this happens in practice even when it is denied verbally. With this device church officials ignore the need for the mediation provided by an analysis of current history, and it ends up auctioning off its solidarity with liberative programs of the poor in history.

As it seeks to maintain a gospel vigilance over the particular course of the struggles of the poor in Central America, the church will have to make use of such analysis of ongoing developments if it is to exercise its solidarity with the poor in a responsible fashion. Ultimately just as the church could not avoid taking a stand on the struggle in Nicaragua, it will not be able to sidestep a historico-theological judgment on the legitimacy or illegitimacy of the concrete movements that provide a channel for the struggles in El Salvador and Guatemala, or on whether it should help put an end to the "terrorist" image that the United States uses to stigmatize them, or on the need to maintain a balanced judgment on processes that indeed cannot avoid all ambiguity, rather than demand of them a conduct that is ethically pure simply because they are revolutionary.

Theologically speaking, once the church has been challenged by taking into account an analysis of ongoing developments, it will have to decide, in vigilance and in solidarity, whether its spiritual wisdom demands that it consider God to be indissolubly bound up with the bourgeois, "democratic" order, or whether it believes that God is ever free and can pronounce a new word in history through the human experience found in a new revolutionary order. The habitual impatience of the church with the ambiguities of any revolutionary process will have to be contrasted—in Central America— with God's patient fidelity to the cause of the poor and to the channels their cause finds in history.

Today in particular the church will have to consider—and several churches, such as those of the United States and Belgium, have already done so—whether, given the intolerance of the United States government with respect to the revolutionary liberation process of the poor in Nicaragua, and given the likelihood of an invasion (blatant or camouflaged), the church, rather than saying nothing, should offer its solidarity in the form of an unmistakably clear denunciation of that possibility.

Finally, in the exercise of solidarity, the churches should be wary of practicing another kind of control, one that takes away from church members, whether lay, religious, or clerical, their inalienable responsibility to deal with these options. Sometimes situations arise in the church where the hierarchy believes its role entails such vigilance that it negates Christian freedom to make a choice between alternatives in history. The flow of material and spiritual goods from one church to another is restricted either through one all-absorbing organization or out of a fear that in their generous solidarity Christians other than bishops might be "manipulated" by "communism." Basically there is a danger of "stifling the Spirit" (1 Thess. 5:19), either because there is an assumption that history is simply repetition and can lead to nothing new, or because persons live by fear rather than by trust in the leaven of Christianity or, finally, because Christians are not regarded as having come of age for judging present history and the options it presents. As we have already discussed, matters would be worse if their purpose were sectarian or if they had a power takeover in mind.

Conclusion: Ecclesial Solidarity, Crisis Point for the Faith of the Church

By way of a brief conclusion, I want to gather together the elements that underly the considerations in this study.

The historical processes to which the poor of Central America are committed today constitute a call for solidarity from the churches that confess their faith in the God and Father of our Lord Jesus Christ. Like any call, like any vocation within the church, these processes test ecclesial faith, force it to exercise discernment, and expose it to critical risk.

The issue at stake is that of treating whole nations in a way that vindicates or negates the God of life. The issue is whether or not the material reality, the palpable flesh, in which the hopes of the afflicted, the marginalized, and the poor are at stake, will be taken seriously or not. No one has seen God: only Jesus of Nazareth has made plain to us the face of God (John 1:18). Today also, Jesus is no longer in our midst (John chap. 14—16, passim). The faith of the first community of disciples was tested in relation to that man, one like any other, son of an artisan everyone knew. His claim to be recognized as the one whose acceptance or rejection entailed life or death was a scandal precisely because his own humanity was so obvious and undeniable, and ultimately so weak. In his attitude of service to the point of giving his life for his friends, others came in contact with an image of the powerful, untouchable, fearful, and unmoving God.

It is to our advantage that he, Jesus of Nazareth, the lord of history, has gone away (John 16:7). Now the scandal is even greater. Now God's face is made plain (to some degree) only in the faces of the crucified multitudes who, with their struggle against all odds, affirm the victory of life over death. It is in relation to these faces, sweaty and bloody from daily struggle, that faith in the Christian God is at stake. The freedom to take on their challenge to human history in solidarity is—as scandalous as it might seem—the freedom of the Spirit, because it is the only freedom that counts, the freedom that is in birth pangs since the beginning of history, the freedom of the children of God. In the present period of grace this has all crystalized in Central America. No one would have had any such suspicion even as early as 1980. God's journey with the poor in history is indeed something unpredictable.

Perhaps the challenge for the churches in the closing years of the twentieth century, a challenge in which their fidelity to the gospel is at stake, is that of bearing, along with the poor, the cause that gives them hope. I say "perhaps" because one cannot speak of God and fidelity to God with absolute sureness. But perhaps solidarity with the poor in their search for liberation in the unfolding of history is today the way to carry out the works that are proper to the kingdom. Perhaps these undertakings are those of the peoples who have suffered in their struggle as few others have: the poor of Guatemala, for example, who are the most forgotten in Central America, and certainly much more forgotten than the people of Poland or Kampuchea, or the refugees who fled Vietnam by boat. Perhaps the churches should undertake solidarity with them all the more inasmuch as given the way the hope of Nicaragua is twisted by those who claim it is out to subvert other countries, and given the silencing of Archbishop Romero, the poor have almost no one to cry out on their behalf or echo their voice. Perhaps (and I shall end on this note) to undertake solidarity with them will mean that the churches will overcome their crisis and do works like those of Jesus and even greater ones (John 14:12). If these "greater works" are not done, perhaps Central America can expect only more war, more hunger, and more unjust exploitive labor.

In any case our hope is in Jesus of Nazareth, the crucified and risen Son of God, whom we believe is the "stronger one" (Luke 11:22), standing up to all the machinations that the "powerful" of this world (Luke 11:21; John 12:31) resort to in order to despoil the poor of Central America of the hope they find in human, Christian, and ecclesial solidarity.

Bibliography

Sources used in preparing these studies have not been cited to support particular points. The following are works that have been most important and most inspirational.

Gonzales Faus, J. I., "Jesús y los demonios: Introducción cristológica a la lucha por la justicia," in *Fe y justicia*, Salamanca, Sígueme, 1981, 61–97.

Gottwald, Norman K., *The Tribes of Yahweh: A Sociology of the Religion of Liberated Israel*, Maryknoll, N.Y., Orbis, 1979.

Gutiérrez, Gustavo, "The Irruption of the Poor in Latin America and the Christian Communities of the Common People," in Torres, Sergio, and Eagleson, John, eds., *The Challenge of Basic Christian Communities*, Maryknoll, N.Y., Orbis, 1981, 107–123

Mateo, J., and Barreto, J., *El Evangelio de Juan: Análisis lingüístico y comentario exegético*, Madrid, Ediciones Cristiandad, 1979.

Metz, Johann Baptist, *Faith in History and Society*, New York, Seabury, 1980. See references to "solidarity" in the index.

Sobrino, Jon, "Dios y los procesos revolucionarios," in *Apuntes para una teología nicaragüense*, San Josè, Costa Rica, DEI, 1981, 105–129.

Martín-Baró, I., and Cardenal, R., eds., *La voz de los sin voz: la palabra viva de Monseñor Romero*, San Salvador, UCA Editores, 1980; Eng. trans., Oscar Romero, *Voice of the Voiceless: The Four Pastoral Letters and Other Statements*, Maryknoll, N.Y., Orbis, 1985.

Other Orbis Titles . . .

CHRIST IN A PONCHO
Witnesses to the Nonviolent Struggles in Latin America
by Adolfo Pérez Esquivel

"A source book on the struggles of the oppressed of Latin America. Along with the moving testimony of this devout Christian layman to peace, nonviolence, and justice, we read the words of the mothers of Argentina, the manifestoes of striking workers, and the pastorals of bishops. This makes for excellent primary source material."

Sojourners

ISBN 0-88344-104-7   *139pp. Paper $6.95*

JESUS CHRIST LIBERATOR
A Critical Christology for Our Time
by Leonardo Boff

"An excellent introduction to the basics of contemporary liberation Christology and thought, written from a position of deep faith."

The Christian Century

"An excellent summary of the development of Christology from Jesus to Chalcedon."   *Library Journal*

ISBN 0-88344-236-1   *335pp. Paper $9.95*

VOICE OF THE VOICELESS
The Four Pastoral Letters and Other Statements
by Archbishop Oscar Romero

"In the complex, tragic, and violent struggle for justice in El Salvador, the Archbishop exemplified what the Latin American bishops at Puebla called 'a preferential option for the poor.' As a pastor he spoke the truth to all in his society, but he spoke *with* and *for* the poor. . . . The assassin's bullet will not silence the power of his words or his witness."

Bishop Thomas C. Kelly, O.P.

ISBN 0-88344-525-5   *208pp. Paper $9.95*

THE WORD REMAINS
A Life of Oscar Romero
by James R. Brockman

"It is unlikely that we shall see a better book about Archbishop Romero. Brockman has been thorough in his research. He writes with personal sympathy about Romero and his development within and in response to the unfolding of the Salvadoran tragedy. He is balanced in his judgments and accurate in his reporting of Salvadoran politics, the poverty and the violence which are the framework of this story." *Catholic Herald*
ISBN 0-88344-364-3 *256pp. Paper $12.95*

THE POWER OF THE POOR IN HISTORY
by Gustavo Gutiérrez

"The essence of Gutiérrez's theology of liberation is evangelical militant compassion, a truly theological project based on the very core of the Gospel. He is the first person in modern history to re-actualize the great Christian themes of theology, starting from a fundamental option for the poor. . . . He conceptualizes not only the pastoral and institutional aspects of Christian ecclesial life but also its dogmatic and ethical aspects, in a way long-forgotten in Europe." *Edward Schillebeeckx*
ISBN 0-88344-388-0 *256pp. Paper $10.95*

WE DRINK FROM OUR OWN WELLS
The Spiritual Journey of a People
by Gustavo Gutiérrez
Preface by Henri Nouwen

"The publication of this book is an extremely significant event in the development of liberation theology. It is the fulfillment of a promise that was implicit in Gutiérrez's *A Theology of Liberation* which appeared in 1971 and soon became the charter for many Latin American theologians and pastoral workers. Gutiérrez realized from the beginning that a theology which is not coming forth from an authentic encounter with the Lord can never be fruitful. It took more than ten years before he had the occasion to fully develop this spirituality, but it was worth waiting for." *Henri Nouwen*

"Gutiérrez has introduced a new spirituality, viz., the spirituality of solidarity with the poor." *Edward Schillebeeckx*
ISBN 0-88344-707-X *176pp. Paper $7.95*

JESUS OF NAZARETH YESTERDAY AND TODAY
Vol. 1: FAITH AND IDEOLOGIES
by Juan Luis Segundo

In his monumental five-volume series, Segundo attempts to place the person and message of Jesus before us all, believer and unbeliever alike. He shakes off the christological dust of previous centuries so that we can hear the words that Jesus spoke.

"Faith and Ideologies continues to develop the key concepts that Segundo had previously analyzed in *The Liberation of Theology.* He does this with great incisiveness and profundity both on the anthropological and the theological levels. A must for those exploring the frontiers of contemporary theology." *Alfred T. Hennelly*

ISBN 0-88344-127-6   *368pp. Paper $14.95*

CHRISTOLOGY AT THE CROSSROADS
A Latin American Approach
by Jon Sobrino

"The most detailed and profound elaboration of a theological method from the perspective of Latin America by a Spanish Jesuit who has worked for many years in Central America. This background appears to have provided him with a perspective that allows a penetrating analysis of both European and Latin theology." *Theological Studies*

"The most thorough study of Christ's nature based on Latin America's liberation theology." *Time*

ISBN 0-88344-076-8   *458pp. Paper $12.95*

SOLIDARITY WITH THE PEOPLE OF NICARAGUA
by James McGinnis

This book is the story of a people. Individual persons, yes, but even more fundamentally it is the story of "the people," the people of Nicaragua. It goes beyond a description of solidarity projects and presents a glimpse of the Nicaraguan Revolution and the process of national reconstruction. Each chapter and each story of Nicaraguan individuals and groups serve as an illustration of some aspect of life in Nicaragua.

The narration is in personal terms—stories—because the basic goal is to foster relationships, to touch hearts and deepen solidarity, so as to lead to more creative, courageous, and perserving political action.

"An excellent combination of resources, analysis, and reflection."

Jim Wallis, Sojourners

ISBN 0-88344-448-8   *192pp. Paper $7.95*

THE PRACTICE OF JESUS
by Hugo Echegaray
Preface by Gustavo Gutiérrez

"The reason why we must begin by looking at social structures in the age of Jesus is that his practice would be unintelligible without reference to the set of objective conditions within which he acted. These conditions not only set the limits within which his ministry was carried on; they also, and above all, supplied a concrete material that became part of the project and message of Christ. The project of Jesus acquired its historical meaning in a dialectical relationship with this set of objective conditions." — *from the book*

ISBN 0-88344-397-X   *176pp. Paper $7.97*

FRONTIERS OF THEOLOGY IN LATIN AMERICA
edited by Rosino Gibellini

"This is the first anthology of essays by South American liberation theologians, and the big names are all here: Gustavo Guriérrez, Hugo Assmann, Juan Luis Segundo, José Míguez Bonino, Enrique Dussel, Rubem Alves, etc. Most of the articles have been freshly written for this volume, and reveal the richness and diversity of this important development in contemporary theology. This volume is essential both as a survey of the basic teachings of liberation theology and as an introduction to its leading advocates. Included are highly useful appendixes with extensive biographical information about the contributors as well as a list of the major publications in this area." *Choice*

ISBN 0-88344-144-6   *333pp. Paper $10.95*

51-9
5-28